Other books by Ingrid Grenon:

*Simply This*
Published by Antrim House Books in Simsbury, Connecticut
www.antrimhousebooks.com/grenon

# LOST MAINE COASTAL SCHOONERS

*From Glory Days to Ghost Ships*

INGRID GRENON

For Donna:

Ingrid

the best neighbor!!!

Charleston London
THE History PRESS

Published by The History Press
Charleston, SC 29403
www.historypress.net

Copyright © 2010 by Ingrid Grenon
All rights reserved
*Front Cover*: Top image courtesy of the Maritime Museum

First published 2010

Manufactured in the United States

ISBN 978.1.59629.956.6

Grenon, Ingrid.
Lost Maine coastal schooners : from glory days to ghost ships / Ingrid Grenon.
p. cm.
Includes bibliographical references.
ISBN 978-1-59629-956-6
1. Shipwrecks--Maine--Atlantic Coast--History--Anecdotes. 2. Schooners--Maine--Atlantic
Coast--History--Anecdotes. 3. Atlantic Coast (Me.)--History, Naval--Anecdotes. 4. Maine--
History, Naval--Anecdotes. I. Title.
F27.A75G74 2010
974.1--dc22
2010008859

*This book is dedicated to my great-great-great-grandfather, Captain William Peachey of Belfast, Maine, master of many schooners and survivor of many shipwrecks; to the English colonists and Maine Wabanaki people from whom I am descended; and to my great-grandfather, Orin Martin, from whom I first learned an appreciation of the sea.*

# Contents

# Acknowledgements

I wish to thank Kimberly Gatto for suggesting that I write this book and Joan Moriarty for her encouragement. I wish also to thank the folks at the Somerset Historical Society, the Boothbay Region Historical Society, the South Portland Historical Society and the Maine Maritime Museum for their assistance with this endeavor and for having patience with me.

I would also especially like to thank Lawrence Lufkin for allowing me to use his wonderful photographs in this book and for his support. For information on Mr. Lufkin's Wiscasset Schooner photography or to order prints, please contact at Lawrence Lufkin, 50 Cherry Lane, Tiverton, Rhode Island, 02878, or at lawrence.lufkin@cox.net.

.

# Being From Maine and Portland Harbor

Although this author was born long after the end of the age of sail, I still got to see what had washed up in its wake. I witnessed its aftereffects, like the debris that comes ashore after a turbulent storm. I found it scattered in bits and pieces all around me like the parts of a puzzle that I would have no hope of envisioning in its entirety—but a puzzle that was captivating nonetheless.

My grandmother's family came from Portland, so off to Portland we would go from time to time to visit her parents. Their house on Portland's Western Promenade was unmistakably Victorian: brick with a tower and a spire. Born during the latter part of the nineteenth century, my great-grandparents were unmistakably Victorian, as well. Interestingly, their home was located within sight of the tomb of the family of the great nineteenth-century poet Henry Wadsworth Longfellow. They occupied the kitchen most often, and the focus of the room was a large window overlooking the Fore River at the mouth of Portland Harbor. That's where my great-grandfather used to sit and watch the ships coming and going.

"Grandpa Martin?" I asked. "How come you always look out the window?"

He turned and smiled. "Well, 'cause there's lots to see."

"What?"

He bent over, picked me up and sat me on his knee. He wore long sleeves and a dark vest with a pocket watch in it. He had a bit of a belly, and his white hair hanged down at the sides of his head. He wore glasses.

"Can't you see what's out there?" he asked.

I looked out the window. It was sunny, and the light came in and flooded the room. "I see boats."

"A-yeah. Boats. Ships. I like to watch them come and go out of the harbor."

I looked. There was something calming about it all: the ocean, the waves, the ships being nudged by tugboats—all seemed to be part of a rhythm.

"When I was a young man, I used to sail out of this harbor to England. Then I purchased apples for a produce company here in Portland. Now I just sit here in this chair and watch the ships come and go."

When I looked out of the window again, I realized why he sat there. I, too, was becoming mesmerized by the view out the window—the rhythm of the sea and the thought of sailing ships and such. For a moment, I wondered. If I tried hard enough, could I see the old sailing ships, too?

Days turned into years, and years into decades, and I still remember my great-grandfather looking out of the window to Portland Harbor and out to the sea. I knew that he was watching the old sailing ships, vessels that had turned to dust, except in his mind. Now it was he who had turned to dust, except in *my* mind. And what of the old ships he had so fondly recalled?

Being from Maine, in proximity to those who have a reverence for the sea, I was spared no detail of my heritage. I recalled hearing stories about the "other" side of the family. The stories were about my great-great-great-grandfather, Captain William Peachey, who was a shipmaster throughout much of the nineteenth century. He was born on Mount Desert Island, Maine, in 1805 and lived in Belfast, Maine, for most of his life. I remembered the ships he lost; one was the schooner *Oneco* that went aground near Cape Hatteras, North Carolina, during a storm in September 1839 with a cargo for Portland. When the wreck was discovered, one man was found dead, lashed to the rigging. Fortunately, the rest of the crew were saved. In particular, I remember a schooner named *General Meade* that was lost on Green Island Ledge near Portland on December 12, 1876, with a cargo bound for Boston. Ancestor Peachey was seventy-one years old then and still a master of schooners.

I imagined that the icy, wintry waters off Portland Harbor in December must have been unbelievably cold. What kind of a man, I wondered, would have wanted to be out at sea that late in his life during an ungodly and frigid New England winter? Could it have been that there on the ocean, standing on the wooden deck of a Maine coastal schooner, he felt the most alive?

I did not appear on this planet until long after the last coasting schooner was scuttled or laid to rest and left to rot. I would not have known of the existence of such ships if I had not been from Maine or if I had not caught a glimpse of the remaining Wiscasset Schooners in their final berth in the summer of 1964 when I was just four years old. There was something about the wooden weather-beaten vessels—ambassadors of another era sitting mired in the muck at low tide—that seized my attention and compelled me to stare.

Never able to shake my fascination with the old four-masted vessels, I would return to Wiscasset from time to time just to visit them and stare at them, spellbound, as I did when I was a child. They were still haunting me. I wrote a book of poetry, *Simply This*, which included a poem entitled "Wiscasset Schooners." What surprised me was the number of people who, after reading or listening to the poem, told me that they had heard of the ships, seen the ships, photographed the ships or simply identified with them in some way.

The schooners continued to haunt me. I knew that I could find no rest until I captured the ships more thoroughly, tried to do them justice somehow or tell their story. I became increasingly interested in Maine commercial schooners of all sorts—not just the type that ancestor Peachey sailed or the four-masted vessels waiting in Wiscasset. What of all the other coastal schooners? What has happened to them? Where are they now? Who were the men who built them and sailed them? Why did they persist for so long into the twentieth century, seemingly trying to forestall the inevitable?

There were many large coastal schooners built in Maine in the latter part of the nineteenth century and even more from 1900 until about 1909, the last arriving during the shipping boom of World War I and just afterward. Hundreds of large schooners were built during this time; this is by no means a history of all of them. It is, instead, the story of only some of the vessels, especially those that lingered.

Because of the many references to Portland Harbor in this book, I wanted to consult an authority on the subject. I visited the South Portland Historical Society at its home near Bug Light, located across from Greater Portland's Eastern Promenade, where the Wiscasset Schooners had rested at anchor in the early '30s. Called "The Bug" due to its small size, it is also known as the Portland Breakwater Light and is located in the harbor near the entrance to Fore River. The station was established in 1855, but the present lighthouse was built in 1875. Before I went inside, I wanted to walk down to the sea and look across the harbor. It was January, and the wind whipped across my face, as if to question my intention. I thought of ancestor Peachey and his shipwreck near that very same harbor in the winter of 1876. I was quite sure that the same wind had challenged him on an infinite number of occasions.

The director of the South Portland Historical Society, Kathryn DiPhilippo, welcomed me and spoke of Portland Harbor.

"I used to sail with my parents in this harbor when I was a child," she explained. "Over there near Fort Gorges, I remember seeing the masts of a ship sticking up out of the water at low tide."

Fort Gorges was named for Sir Ferdinando Gorges, deemed the Lord Proprietor of Maine by King James I of England. Although he never set foot in the New World, Gorges was a sponsor of the Waymouth Expedition in 1605 and a sponsor of Popham Colony in 1607, both in Maine. In 1623, King James granted six thousand acres of land to Christopher Levett, an associate of Gorges's, so that he would establish an English colony there. The six thousand acres of land, known as *Machigonne* or "Great Neck" by the Wabanaki people who inhabited the area, is known today as Portland Harbor and Casco Bay. Levett left the colony after only one year, leaving some of his men behind. They were never heard from again.

Subsequent attempts to settle the area were eventually successful, despite the many times that they were destroyed and then rebuilt. In 1676, the village was annihilated by the Wabanaki people in King Philip's War, it was demolished again in 1690 during King William's War and it was shelled and burned by the British in 1775 during the Revolutionary War. In 1866, much of Portland was again destroyed by fire, this time through carelessness during a Fourth of July celebration. Portland was then rebuilt with brick, taking on a distinctly Victorian appearance, which it retains today. The image on Portland's city seal is that of a phoenix rising from ashes, with the accompanying motto *Resurgam*, Latin for "I will rise again." This is certainly apt, as Portland has become the largest city in the state of Maine.

History is made daily, and what is more recent replaces that which came before it, coming to us and leaving like the ebb and flow of the tides—or of time itself. The last remnants of an earlier age are all but gone, and this author who first glimpsed them as a small child is now a half-century old. It is time, again, to recount the story of the Wiscasset Schooners and their brethren.

# The *Virginia of Sagadahoc* and Popham Colony

T he majesty of the great sailing vessels…the romance and reality of a life made at sea, with its breathtaking beauty, absolute tranquility and furious, raging tempests…the square-riggers, Downeasters and, especially, the schooners…the men who built them and the men who sailed them…the jagged, rock-strewn coastline…all of these defined Maine for so long.

To fully appreciate the culmination, the peak, and then the inevitable decline, we must first envision the phenomenon as a whole, from beginning to end. There were shipbuilders in Maine long before there were Pilgrims at Plymouth. There were English shipbuilders in Maine in August 1607, thirteen years before the group that included the Pilgrims landed at what was to become the Plymouth Colony and just a few months after the settlement of Jamestown.

The rugged territory of Maine, way back when it was known as Northern Virginia, was a wild, unexplored wilderness laden with native peoples and primeval forests. It was these very forests, and the possibility of a lucrative fur and precious metal trade, that interested King James I of England and his recently established Virginia Company of Plymouth. The intention of this business venture was to determine if the resources in this New World were exploitable.

In the summer of 1605, an expedition of twenty-nine men sent by prominent investors came ashore at what is now known as Monhegan Island, Maine, and slowly moved up the coast. Intending to land a bit farther south, a storm threw their vessel *Archangel* off course and into the Gulf of Maine. This expedition was led by Captain George Waymouth, who had been engaged by Sir John Popham, chief justice of England; Henry Wriothesley, the Earl of Southampton; Sir Ferdinando Gorges; and Sir Thomas Arundel.

Waymouth's mission was to evaluate the area for settlement and availability of resources. The members of the expedition befriended the "savages," as they called them, just long enough to gain their confidence, learn the lay of the land and determine that the resources in this place would indeed be of use to the king. According to expedition member James Rosier's seventeenth-century account of the voyage, the natives invited the Englishmen to sit by the fire on the beach and smoke their tobacco. Interestingly, the pipe was the short claw of a lobster. Unfortunately, just before setting sail for home, the English abducted five Wabanaki men and took them back to England for display.

Captain Waymouth's visit to the New World was considered a success, and plans for a colony were soon underway. On August 13, 1607, accommodating winds brought two ships and more than one hundred colonists from England across the Atlantic to the shores of what is now known as the state of Maine. They came to develop trade and make use of the dense forests by establishing a shipbuilding colony. The leader of this contingent was George Popham, nephew of Sir John Popham. (Sir John Popham was also among the financial backers of the venture.) Second in command was Raleigh Gilbert, nephew of Sir Walter Raleigh. It was the *Gift of God* that arrived at the mouth of what the Wabanaki people called the Sagadahoc (today's Kennebec River) carrying Popham and his crew, and it was the *Mary and John* that brought Gilbert a few days later with the remainder of the group.

It is ironic that Popham's ship was called the *Gift of God*, as the Wabanaki people indigenous to the area certainly didn't regard them as such. The dishonorable actions of Captain Waymouth and his party only a few years earlier had irrevocably stained the image of the European visitors and sealed the fate of colonization in that area for years to come.

The first order of business at the newly established Popham Colony (located just ten miles away from present-day Bath, Maine) was to build a stronghold. This effort culminated in the erection of the star-shaped Fort St. George, which included a storehouse, an admiral's house, a cooperage, a buttery and a chapel. The nine canons were strategically placed. Perhaps after all of this, the shipbuilders began their painstaking work. One can only imagine the sorts of preparations that were being made, or not being made, as the summer was soon to come to an abrupt end. How could these Englishmen possibly have fathomed the severity of the winter yet to come?

Historical records that depict daily life and conditions at the colony are incredibly scant. Fortunately, I have in my possession a limited edition of the *History of Kennebec County, Maine*, published in 1892. This rare volume includes transcripts from Captain Raleigh Gilbert's logbook, made by the actual clerk of Popham Colony, Robert Davies, who was no doubt with

Gilbert at the time these events were taking place. Apparently, by September 23, 1607, the colony leaders believed that they were adequately fortified enough to begin exploring the area farther up the river. The record states that Captain Gilbert and nineteen men took their shallop to sail for the head of the Sagadahoc River. It was during this trip that the group met the Wabanaki people for the first time since they had arrived. It is described here in excerpts from Gilbert's original logbook, taken from the *Historie of Travaile into Virginia* compiled by William Strachey, as reprinted in the *History of Kennebec County, Maine*:

> *They sayled all this daye, and the 24th the like untill six of the clock in the afternoone, when they landed on the river's side, where they found a champion land* {camping ground}, *and very fertile, where they remayned all that night; in the morning they departed from thence and sayled up the river and came to a flatt low island where ys a great cataract or downfall of water, which runneth by both sides of this island very shold and swift…They haled their boat with a strong rope through this downfall perforce, and went near a league further up, and here they lay all night; and in the first of the night there called certain savages on the further side of the river unto them in broken English; they answered them againe and parled* {talked} *long with them, when towards morning they departed.* [Note: There were many English-speaking visitors who came to trade and explore, including the Waymouth party, from whom the Wabanaki would learn the language]. *In the morning there came a sagamo* [highest level of chief or regional leader] *called his name Sebenoa, and told us how he was lord of the river Sachadehoc.*

The excerpts from the logbook continue, describing events that clearly show that the Wabanaki were wary of the colonists. Despite this, Sebenoa did invite them to a nearby village. A reader is not sure, however, if this was a friendly gesture or an attempt by the Wabanaki to show their ability to defend themselves if necessary. The log continues:

> *And after a good tedious march, they came indeed at length unto those salvages' howses wheere* {they} *found neere fifty able men very strong and tall, such as their like before they had not seene; all newly painted and armed with their bowes and arrowes.*

Eventually, there is some exchanging of merchandise and then some trouble with the colonist's firelocks, of which the Wabanaki seemed fearful. This resulted in both sides taking up arms:

*Captain Gilbert caused the musquettiers to present {aim} their peeces, the which, the salvages seeing, presently let go the boat rope and betook them to their bowes and arrowes, and ran into the bushes, nocking their arrowes, but did not shoot, neither did ours at them.*

Finally, from the text of the *History of Kennebec County, Maine* there comes a description of the events that occurred when the colonists had departed from the company of the Wabanaki and were returning back to the fort:

*There, the next morning (Sunday, September 27), they performed the ceremony of taking possession of the country for their king, by erecting in his name the cross of Christianity at the place where they had twice lodged. Thus leaving the sacred emblem standing as the official vestige of their visit, they departed. It would be interesting to know precisely the spot where the cross was planted, and how long it remained as an object of awe to the savages. We never hear more of Sebenoa; he was the first in the long line of Kennebec chiefs whose names have been preserved in the white man's annals; his dust, with that of his beloved warriors who posed so grandly before their visitors, has long mingled with the mold of the forest where he reigned, but his peaceful welcome to the white strangers who earliest set foot on the soil of the capital of Maine, invests his name with a charm that will preserve it while the language of the race that has supplanted his own is spoken or read.*

After reading the material contained in the logbook, one must wonder where Captain Popham was and why was he so conspicuously absent from these treks into the wilderness. In February, five months after Captain Gilbert's first encounter with the Wabanaki in the forest and before winter was over, George Popham died. His was the only death in the colony that bore his name. Rumored to have been in poor health, one can only imagine that the frigid winter in this part of the New World had taken its toll. Captain Raleigh Gilbert became the new president of the colony.

The weather must have been unbelievably bitter; the glacial wind coming off the ocean and tearing down the river would certainly have been biting and unforgiving. Records show that the Kennebec River froze over that year. This was a winter the likes of which the English had never experienced before and could never have imagined. The colonists arrived in mid-August, with no time to plant or develop stores for the bleak season to come. The piercing wind no doubt whined, whipped and punished the strangers whose tread on the earth showed no reverence for it. The same wind had tossed and

The pinnace *Virginia of Sagadahoc*.
*Courtesy of Maine Maritime Museum.*

tempered the Wabanaki, making them strong. Wary of these newcomers, however, the Wabanaki people were not anxious to help. In December, it is no wonder that half of the settlers went back to England on the *Gift of God*.

The remaining forty-five stayed on and were determined to continue, despite the arrival of a supply ship that brought the news that Sir John Popham had died. It wasn't until the next supply ship arrived with news that Captain Raleigh Gilbert's brother had died, leaving him his entire estate, that the future of the colony took a downward turn. Gilbert and the remaining colonists decided to return to England in the fall of 1608, just over a year after they had arrived.

They left on two vessels, the *Mary and John*, on which they had come, and the newly built *Virginia of Sagadahoc*, a thirty-ton pinnace. It is believed that the vessel was just less than fifty feet in length, with a beam of nearly fifteen feet. The *Virginia of Sagadahoc* proved quite seaworthy and was recorded to have made at least one other voyage across the Atlantic.

Lasting only one year and often referred to as New England's "Lost Colony," Popham did manage to establish Maine as the site of the first European shipbuilding colony in the New World. Interestingly, it was located only ten miles from present-day Bath, Maine, long heralded as the largest and most prolific shipbuilding town on the Northeast coast, especially famous for its production of coastal schooners.

# Early Schooners and the
# Advent of Steam

While the colonists at Popham Colony were building the *Virginia of Sagadahoc*, the Dutch were designing the first schooners. Schooners traditionally were fore- and aft-rigged vessels with two or more masts, the mainmast being the second and larger of the two. The number of masts eventually grew as the need for cargo space increased. The vessels differed from the more prevalent square-rigged craft not only in the structure of their sails, but also because they were easier to operate and required a much smaller crew.

It is the Dutch who are credited for building the first fore- and aft-rigged ships, as there is artwork in existence that depicts such vessels dating back to about 1600. The word "schooner," however, is reputed to have had its origins in New England just after the turn of the following century.

Schooner history really begins in Gloucester, Massachusetts, according to lore. In 1713, Gloucester shipbuilder Andrew Robinson launched a new type of vessel with fore- and aft-rigged sails. The new design quickly became popular and soon became the choice among fishermen in the area, putting Gloucester on the map as a primary fishing town. When the new ship slid gracefully into the water, a bystander is reputed to have exclaimed, "Oh, how she scoons!" To this comment Robinson is said to have replied, "Then a schooner let her be." The word *scoon* itself originated in Scotland and means "to skim over water."

Three-masted schooners became quite popular by the middle of the nineteenth century and remained in use well after the turn of the next century. Three-masted (or "tern") schooners were also especially popular in

The configuration of sails on this square-rigged whaling bark clearly shows the contrast between it and a "schooner" (fore- and aft-rigged vessel). *Author's collection.*

Nova Scotia. Later, their larger American brethren were deemed by many Canadian seafarers to be too unwieldy and excessive.

By the latter part of the nineteenth century, traditional two- and three-masted commercial schooners had been around for quite a while. There were also a great many fishing schooners all along the coasts of New England and the Canadian Maritimes. In the shipbuilding town of Essex, Massachusetts, thousands of fishing schooners were launched. Even the famous Gloucester, Massachusetts fishing fleets were composed of many schooners that were built in Essex. There was more going on than fishing, though. After the Civil War, the era of industrialization was ushered in by technology and mechanization. America was coming of age, and the rural, pastoral setting that had dominated much of the country for so long would soon be lost forever, at least in the larger cities and towns. The railroads were expanding, telegraph and eventually telephone would revolutionize communication and machines were taking the places of horses and men. This transformation increased the need for shipping.

A three-masted schooner harnesses the wind, heavily laden with lumber and under full sail. *Author's collection.*

Steam power was around and had been ever since its introduction in the latter part of the seventeenth century. Only one of many progenitors of the idea, James Watt invented his version in 1765. In 1804, Richard Trevithick successfully tested the world's first steam railway locomotive in Wales. In 1825, George Stephenson built the world's first public railway in Britain. America's first steam railroads were built in 1827 in Quincy, Massachusetts, to haul granite and in Mauch Chunk, Pennsylvania, to transport coal.

In 1819, the *Savannah*, a full-rigged sailing ship, was converted to steam use. With the addition of a ninety-horsepower engine, a boiler and a paddle wheel, the ninety-eight-foot-long and twenty-five-foot-wide *Savannah* was ready for use. The master of the vessel, Captain Moses Rogers, was anxious to dispel any fears that the public had over steam-powered vessels and supervised the installation of the machinery. The *Savannah*'s maiden voyage with her new steam engine began on March 28 as she headed out of New York Harbor bound for Savannah, Georgia. President James Monroe, who was visiting nearby, inspected the vessel and dined aboard, enthusiastic about the new technology.

On May 22, 1819, the *Savannah* left her homeport in Georgia bound for Liverpool, England. Her arrival at Liverpool twenty-nine days later on June

20 marked the first ocean crossing of a steam-propelled vessel. The *Savannah* was only steam-assisted, and she only made approximately 16 percent of the Atlantic crossing using steam power. Interestingly, her steam equipment was removed shortly afterward, and she was converted back to sail. It would seem that the technology wasn't quite good enough to make a voyage economical, and most of the space aboard ship was utilized to carry the seventy-five tons of coal and twenty-five cords of wood necessary to run the boiler.

As early as 1815, mariners in Maine were experimenting with steam-propelled seagoing craft, although most were failures. By the mid-1820s, however, there was regular steamboat service to some Maine ports. The schooner-rigged steamboat *Legislator* made regular runs between Portland and Boston in 1825. Others soon followed, and steam and sail packets were quite common by the middle part of the century.

The *Royal William*, a wooden-hulled Canadian steamer that was equipped with masts and sails, crossed the Atlantic using just steam in 1833. The first crossings using vessels designed exclusively for steam came in 1838 when two competing British steamship companies sent the *Great Western* and the *Sirius* across the Atlantic. The first vessel to use a propeller instead of a paddle wheel was the *Archimedes* in 1840. The *Great Britain* in 1845 was the first iron steamship to cross the Atlantic using a propeller. It is important to note that all of these early steamships were still equipped with auxiliary masts and sails.

It wasn't until the latter part of the nineteenth century that steam began to seriously contend with sail. Paradoxically, however, it was at this time that the steam hoisting engines used in sailing vessels for deck work enabled commercial sail to remain viable through the early part of the twentieth century.

The advantages of a large schooner compared to a square-rigged vessel or a steamship were simple: the schooner required a much smaller crew and cost less. A full crew for a typical four-masted schooner would have numbered nine. Usually, this would include the master, his first mate, a steam engineer to operate the hoisting equipment, a cook and five able-bodied seamen. A full-rigged vessel of the same size would have needed about twenty-three seamen, and a steamer would have required an even larger crew. Wooden schooners were also cheaper to manufacture and operate, could be loaded more quickly and had more space for cargo. The use of steam "donkey" engines would provide the power to raise the sails and hoist the anchors. Later, gasoline-powered hoisting engines further added to the economy of a schooner by eliminating the need for a licensed steam engineer.

Bill of Lading for schooner heading from Boston to Wiscasset, Maine, in 1860, specifically stating that goods will be delivered in good condition "the danger of the Seas only excepted." *Author's collection.*

Two prominent Maine shipbuilders out for a drive on Popham Beach. Standing in the foreground is William Donnell and seated in the buggy are his wife, Clara, and their children; behind them are Gardner Deering and his wife, Lydia. *Courtesy of Maine Maritime Museum.*

# From Glory Days to Ghost Ships

The reason why large schooner-rigged commercial ships became so popular so quickly in an age that was fast being overtaken by steam-powered vessels was due to economics. It was cheaper to use a wind-driven wooden vessel equipped with steam-powered auxiliary machinery and have a much smaller crew, and in the United States there were innovative shipbuilders ready to meet the demand. Well, meet it they did, and they continued right up into the early part of the twentieth century. Most of these shipbuilders were from Maine, and mostly from Bath, Maine, located only about ten miles upriver from where the very first ship was built in 1608.

What kind of men were they? One does not need to have known them personally to venture a guess. One needs only to know of the place from which they sprung and the story of the schooners. While the West was being won on another frontier, these were men who tried their hands at harnessing the sea by building ships on which to ride on it. They were heroes and incurable romantics but also a practical, sensible sort of folk. They were tough, stalwart and resolute—tempered by the land they had tamed. These were men who managed to forestall the end of an era, keep commercial sail viable well into the twentieth century and even make a little money besides.

# Schooners Come of Age

## The Four-Masters

By the 1880s, the face of the country was changing, and its habits were growing. The need for coal as an energy source was increasing. Thomas Edison had a lot to do with it, and electricity was literally taking America by storm. A commercial power station located in Lower Manhattan began operations in September 1882, and it didn't take long for this technology to reach coastal Maine. By December 31, 1888, for instance, the city of Belfast, Maine, was lighted by electricity. It was found that wheels powered by water were not sufficient to run the dynamos (generators), and so steam engines were adopted. The demand for coal to power the steam engines that ran the dynamos, and therefore produce electricity, increased tremendously during this time. With the expansion of the railroad, West Virginia coal could now be transported economically via railway to ports in Virginia. Once the coal got to the coast by rail, it needed a way to get up to the ports along the northeast coasts of New England and the Canadian Maritimes, thus ushering in the age of the large coastal schooners, which were designed primarily to be colliers.

The phenomenon of the large "coasters" began with the four-masters, the first built in 1880 and the last in 1921. During this period, several hundred four-masted schooners were built, over 450 on the East Coast and about 325 of these in Maine. They were quite capable of deep-sea travel, and many met their violent ends far from the shores of the United States. Designed especially to carry large quantities of coal, these vessels also transported lumber, oil, fertilizer, logwood (used to make dye), resin, salt, ice, molasses and anything else they could pack into the hold—including, on rare occasions, bootleg whiskey.

The first true four-masted schooner was the *William L. White*, built in Bath, Maine, by Goss & Sawyer and launched in July 1880. She was built for Jacob Phillips of Taunton, Massachusetts. She was 205 feet long on deck and 40 feet wide. Her length from jib boom to spanker boom was 309 feet, and she carried 5,017 yards of sail. The *White* was also equipped with a ten-horsepower steam engine for hoisting sails, raising anchor, pumping and discharging cargo when necessary. She was designed to carry nearly 1,500 tons of coal. Her four masts were named—fore, main, mizzen and spanker—and her launching signaled the beginning of the age of the big coasters, lasting over forty years and encroaching into the early 1920s. The following is an excerpt from the *Boston Advertiser* of September 20, 1880:

> *The four-masted schooner William L. White, of Taunton, now lies at the North End, discharging coal. She is the first vessel carrying four fore-and-aft sails that ever entered this port, and the only one, thus far, constructed for the coastwise trade and for sea-going.*

The *William L. White*, on her maiden voyage, took a cargo of ice from the Kennebec to Washington, D.C., and returned to New Bedford, Massachusetts, with a load of coal. Unfortunately, although she got a good start, she didn't last very long. Early in the morning on November 19, 1882, off the coast of Pennsylvania, the *White* met the same fate as many of her brethren when she was rammed by a steamer. The officer on the deck of the steamship *Algiers* saw the schooner's light only moments before impact. When the steamer's light revealed the sails and spars of the schooner, it was too late. Although the engines were immediately reversed, the steamer hit the schooner just abaft her fore rigging, cutting the ship nearly in two. The *William L. White* quickly sank with her cargo, but the crew was rescued.

Since there were literally hundreds of four-masted schooners built on both the West and East Coasts, and even more if you include those that were built for use on the Great Lakes, it would be impossible to depict the careers of all of them. Instead, I will portray only those ships that were built in Maine or that had something to do with Maine. I will also focus on those ships whose careers were lengthy or that somehow managed to exist in some form long after the age of sail had come to an end. The most famous of these four-masted schooners, the *Luther Little* and the *Hesper*, will be discussed in another chapter.

The four-masted *Anna R. Heidritter*, built in Bath as the *Cohasset*, was first launched in 1903. On January 22, 1907, while in Baltimore Harbor, she

The *Anna Heidritter* lying idle. *Author's collection.*

burned to the waterline. She was rebuilt in Maryland, like the mythical phoenix that rose up from its ashes, and relaunched as the *Anna R. Heidritter* in 1910. In 1918, during a trip to the Mediterranean, she survived a U-boat attack that took one of her masts out and left bullet fragments in the remaining masts. Luckily, she was noticed by a British warship and towed to safety.

In 1919, just after the end of World War I, Captain Bennett Coleman from Cotuit, Massachusetts, became the master of the *Heidritter*. There is an interesting parallel between Bennett Coleman and this ship that he would

The deck on the *Anna Heidritter. Author's collection.*

captain for twenty-two years. To start, Captain Coleman survived three near tragic disasters at sea. The first occurred early in his career when his schooner, the *George Edmonds*, caught fire and burned at sea. He and his crew drifted in an open lifeboat for over a week before they were rescued, but they managed to survive the ordeal. The final and more poignant parallel comes at the end of the careers of both boat and man.

In November 1928, bound from Charleston, South Carolina, to New York with a load of lumber, the *Heidritter* sent out an SOS and was in danger, the *New York Times* reported. The steamship *K.R. Kingsbury* reported passing the ship, which was flying signals of distress. The *Kingsbury* also reported that the *Heidritter* had lost her lifeboat and provisions and had been blown far off course by the storm that battered her, as she was about thirty miles off the coast of Florida. Luckily, she made it back to port. In February 1936, laden with 1,200 tons of coal for Charleston, South Carolina, the *Heidritter* was caught in a nasty gale and blown off course again. By the time the Coast Guard cutter *Yamacraw* found her, the ship had lost her sails and the crew was out of water. The *Heidritter* was again taken in tow by a Coast Guard cutter, this time in November 1937. The cutter *Champlain* towed the four-masted schooner into New York after she collided with the 16,000-ton Red Star liner SS *Pennland*.

By the time World War II began, the *Heidritter* was one of the last four-masted schooners still remaining in service, and she was getting a bit long

Looking toward the bow on the *Anna Heidritter*'s deck. *Author's collection.*

in the tooth, as was Captain Coleman. She made more and more trips out to the West Indies with coal, returning with whatever she could, usually logwood or manure for fertilizer. After a particularly difficult passage north from Venezuela, carrying fertilizer for Charleston, both the *Heidritter* and her master were battered in a storm, the former having lost some of her sails and the captain some of his nerve. They both arrived in Charleston on March 13, 1941.

Bennett Coleman was enjoying a brief retirement in February 1942 when he was asked to take command of the *Heidritter* one more time. Her new master had suddenly become ill, had put in at Charleston with his cargo of logwood and was unable to continue to Pennsylvania, his destination. Captain Coleman, now seventy-five years old, likely did not hesitate to take his place back on the deck of his beloved schooner. On February 25, the ship left Charleston bound for Pennsylvania. The experienced captain knew that in order to be safe from German submarine attacks he would have to sail dangerously near the coast. He also knew that to do so put his ship at risk, as it would be difficult to keep the vessel from running aground in the event of a storm. Without an engine, she would be at the mercy of the weather.

Near Cape Hatteras, the dreaded vessel graveyard, the *Anna R. Heidritter* did meet with a sinister mounting gale. It happened on March 2, 1942, and she was caught too close to shore when the storm began to blow. Despite all efforts from crew and captain, the *Heidritter* went aground on Ocracoke, near

Hatteras, North Carolina, and broke her back. The crew lashed themselves to the masts to weather the storm, and the valiant men from the Hatteras Lifesaving Station rescued them all.

Captain Coleman returned to the broken ship after the storm subsided to retrieve his personal belongings and pay his respects. He was saddened by the loss of his cherished sailing vessel and knew that there would be none to replace her. She was the last of her kind. Ironically, one week later, on March 12, 1942, Captain Coleman took a taxi through Newark, New Jersey, to visit relatives. In a freak accident, the taxi he was riding in bumped the car in front of it. Captain Coleman fell forward at the impact and broke his neck, dying instantly. Neither the taxi nor the vehicle it hit was damaged in any way.

Originally built in 1919 by the J.H. Price Shipbuilding Company in Seattle, Washington, the four-masted *Snetind* was, at first, a West Coast schooner. At over 234 feet long and just over 45 feet wide she was a good-sized four-master, but she was quite a bit different from anything originating in New England. Considered a "baldheaded" schooner, the *Snetind* carried no topmasts and was also equipped with an auxiliary gasoline engine. The story of the *Snetind* is remarkable because, not long after her launching, she was purchased by Joseph W. Gorman of Worcester, Massachusetts, and sent to the Percy & Small Shipyard in Bath to be "rebuilt." Oddly enough, her rebuilding included the removal of the gasoline engine and her re-rigging with topmasts! Unbelievably, late in 1920 the Percy & Small folks turned back the hands of time and refitted the large ship with a manner of rigging already considered antiquated for a commercial vessel. By 1920, the wooden shipbuilding industry was, unfortunately, coming to an end, albeit a belated end due to World War I. In Bath, the Percy & Small Shipyard was busy repairing and refitting vessels, although it was not turning out any new ones. Interestingly, the *Snetind* was the last big schooner to leave the Percy & Small yard.

In the early 1920s, the *Snetind* was kept busy in the coal and lumber trades along the East Coast, like many of her kind that still remained in service. In January 1923, she was caught in a winter storm that blew her headsails away while lying off Cape Cod heavily laden with 2,300 tons of coal. The beginning of the end of the *Snetind's* sailing days came in November 1927 after she departed from Norfolk, Virginia, her hold full of coal for Bangor, Maine. She tangled with a fierce storm that tore her sails and brought down part of her rigging as she struggled with the seas. She was assisted by Coast Guard cutter *Manning* and was towed back into port, where she remained under repair for six weeks. After the extensive repairs were completed, she again set sail and headed north for Maine. Ten days out and approaching

Provincetown, Massachusetts, an insurmountable problem became evident. The coal in *Snetind*'s hold, which had been there for months, was ablaze. It took two tugs and a navy vessel to put out the fire, after which the schooner was towed into Boston Harbor, where her coal was discharged. She was not repaired but was instead laid up at a wharf in East Boston. It was 1928.

The *Snetind*'s story was by no means finished; in many respects it had just begun, although her sailing career was at an end. The schooner was left to sit idle by a wharf in East Boston for a few years. It was common practice to pay a ship watchman to stay aboard unused vessels to keep them tidy and in good repair and to keep vandals and looters out. By 1931, the *Snetind*'s owners allowed a woman and her son to live aboard the schooner, which was looking pretty abandoned. Mrs. Ann Winsor Sherwin, formerly of Long Island, was the divorced wife of author and playwright Louis Sherwin. She had clearly decided to withdraw from fashionable society.

In January 1936, the *Snetind*'s owners decided to scuttle her, as it had become quite clear that she would be of no further use to them, and they no longer

The *Snetind* on November 12, 1927, after a bout with a nasty gale that would end her sailing days. *Author's collection.*

wanted to pay her wharf fees. The *Snetind*'s occupants refused to leave, despite the many efforts that were made to evict them. Soon the battle became famous, and the newspapers kept their readers up-to-date, some no doubt siding with the schooner's lodgers. Left with no other course of action, the schooner's owners, now the Montgomery Navigation Company, towed the *Snetind* into the harbor and anchored her, surrendering all responsibility to Mrs. Sherwin. Unfortunately, not too long afterward a strong winter gale tore across the harbor and ripped the schooner and her inhabitants away from their mooring during the middle of the night. Perhaps her last voyage, the *Snetind* grounded near Spectacle Island in Boston Harbor, four miles offshore from downtown. What a ghostly sight she must have been, silently moving across the harbor in the pitch black of a stormy night, derelict and without sails.

With the schooner now aground on Spectacle Island, police boats were the only way the tenants could get to shore. Despite cries from health officials, unbelievably, the mother and son were not removed from the ship. As the years continued to pass, the schooner's seams began to leak, the tides rising and falling within her as well as without. Far away from Boston Harbor and the forsaken schooner, a battle was raging: World War II. Mrs. Sherwin's son finally had to leave the ship in 1943 when he was drafted. Shortly after, Mrs. Sherwin became ill and was taken to a hospital.

During much of 1947, the *Snetind*'s four masts were still standing. On August 31, after a suspicious cabin cruiser was observed near the vessel, flames were seen leaping from the schooner. Despite the fact that a fireboat was sent to the scene, there was no attempt to put out the fire. Recognizable as only a hulk and deemed to be a menace to navigation, the *Snetind* languished until July 21, 1951, when she was towed into deep water and sunk. It was noted, before she went down, that some flowers the Sherwins had planted were still blooming on her blackened deck. The *Snetind* was the last large wooden-hulled commercial sailing vessel ever to lie in Boston Harbor.

One might think that her descent into the murky depths of Boston Harbor was the end of the *Snetind*, but it was not. Unbelievably, even in the twenty-first century, the *Snetind* still has many visitors even though she lies deep underwater. She has become quite a popular spot for scuba divers who want to visit "shipwreck" sites. This is certainly an unusual story for a ship with an unusual name. A bit of research revealed the likely origin of the name *Snetind*. In the Arctic Circle, in Norway, the Svartisen (or "Black Ice") Glacier lies in the largest ice field in northern Scandinavia; its highest peak is called "Snetind." The name is perhaps fitting for a ship that would be forever entombed beneath black, icy waters at the bottom of Boston Harbor.

# A Few Five-Masters

O nly eight years after the first four-master dipped her stern into the Kennebec River, the five-master was born. Oddly enough, these immense coastal schooners, the last vestiges of the age of sail, were truly a phenomenon of the industrial revolution as well as a result of the ingenuity of Maine shipbuilders.

More than forty five-masted schooners were built on the East Coast, and most of those were built in Maine. I will relay the stories of some of them, sorting through the residue of that last magnificent era of sail, trying to piece it together with the resources at hand.

Launched on December 1, 1888, the *Governor Ames* has the distinction of being the first five-masted oceangoing schooner ever built on the East Coast, and she was constructed at the Storer Shipyard in Waldoboro, Maine. It is interesting that this history-making first five-masted schooner was built in Maine for the Atlantic Shipping Company located in Somerset, Massachusetts. The *Governor Ames*, named after the governor of Massachusetts, was an impressive 265 feet long and nearly 50 feet wide and could carry three thousand tons of coal. She was a thing of beauty that rode the seas as gracefully as a ballerina, and she was practical. Much of her beauty did lie in her practicality. The *Governor Ames* is covered more thoroughly in another chapter.

The story of the five-masted *Cora F. Cressy* is certainly an interesting one. She was 273 feet long and 45 feet wide and was launched on April 12, 1902, from the Percy & Small Shipyard in Bath, Maine. Actually, it was her final career that was unique in comparison to her former life as a collier.

From Glory Days to Ghost Ships

The *Governor Ames. Courtesy of Somerset Historical Society.*

Aside from a few collisions and suffering from the ups and downs of the coal market, the *Cressy*'s career was rejuvenated somewhat, along with many other big coasters, during World War I. Her reputation as a stalwart vessel of the sea peaked in the '20s when, in March 1924, she survived a horrific storm off Pollock Rip near Vineyard Haven, Massachusetts, that claimed the famous *Wyoming* and another schooner. The sole survivor of the furious gale, the *Cressy* limped back into her homeport of Portland, Maine, a little beat up but clearly salvageable. It was speculated that her unusually high bow allowed her to ride the turbulent seas so well. After this, she was hailed as the "Queen of the Atlantic Seaboard."

In the latter part of the decade, the *Cora F. Cressy* fell prey to a number of unfortunate incidents. In 1926, the *Cressy* was towed into port after her captain was killed when he fell through one of the hatches. In August 1928, with Captain John Brown as her master, the *Cressy* had trouble with a hurricane. She sailed from Hampton Roads, Virginia, into Portland Harbor with her mainsail lost. The wooden schooner was laid up due to the high cost of repairs, and things got worse. The *Cressy* was purchased by Boston entrepreneurs and towed into Boston on January 26, 1929, by the tug *Nathaniel Doane*. A covering was built over her deck, and she was converted into a nightclub and moored off Nantasket and then Gloucester, Massachusetts. She was then renamed *Levaggi's Showboat*. It was rumored

The *Cora F. Cressy* riding a squall; the photo was taken from the starboard side, looking astern. *Courtesy of Maine Maritime Museum.*

that she was a speakeasy, which was likely true, as her career as a floating entertainment palace seemed to wane after Prohibition was repealed in 1933. In 1935, she was towed into Providence, Rhode Island, for one final season as a club and then towed back to Boston to lie at a wharf.

Finally, in 1938, the *Cressy* was sold again and towed back to Maine to be used as a lobster storage facility. Because her hull was too strong for numerous holes to be drilled to allow a fresh flow of water for the lobsters, the *Cressy* was used as a breakwater instead. For years she lay on the Medomak River in Bremen, Maine, as a breakwater beside a lobster pound, not far from where the very first five-masted schooner was built. The story does not end here, however, and the *Cressy* survived right into the twenty-first century, the sole remnant of a once numerous fleet of coastal schooners, just as she was the sole survivor of the Gale of 1926 that hit Pollock Rip. Unbelievably, in 1990, the *Cressy* was listed on the National Register of Historic Places, a testament to her builders and to the end of the great age of sailing vessels.

The *Kineo* was the only steel-hulled five-masted schooner ever built and was launched at the shipyard of Arthur Sewall & Company in Bath in 1903. The *Kineo* was 259 feet long and could carry three thousand tons of cargo.

36

Once hailed as "Queen of the Atlantic Seaboard," the once magnificent five-masted schooner *Cora F. Cressy* as she appeared in 1972, a stripped hulk in a cove in Bremen, Maine. *Courtesy of Maine Maritime Museum.*

She was equipped with a steam boiler that provided the power to raise the sails and move heavy objects on deck, as well as heat the cabins. There was usually plenty of coal available, but it was often difficult to find fresh water to run the large boiler. Often the scuppers were blocked and the rainwater salvaged for use in the boiler.

Between 1905 and 1906, the *Kineo* made an ill-fated voyage around the world with Frank W. Patten as her master. Captain Patten certainly had a fine reputation as an able master of ships, and this was not disputed, but he was more experienced sailing square-riggers than schooners, and the trials that the *Kineo* and her crew endured over the long journey were numerous. In January 1905, she departed Norfolk, Virginia, loaded with over 2,700 tons of coal bound for use by the U.S. Navy in newly acquired Manila, where entrepreneurs were eyeing the possibility of a lucrative coal market. Confident that the journey would bear good fortune, with his wife and young daughter aboard Patten headed for Manila in the Philippines via the Cape of Good Hope, the route commonly taken by square-rigged vessels.

The schooner-rigged *Kineo* had difficulty with the sort of gales she encountered in that part of the open sea. Her constant rolling was aggravating to Captain Patten, who no doubt wished that he had some square sails to keep her stable. To further add to the difficulty, a schooner's sails are handled from the deck rather than from aloft as in square-rigged vessels. With the deck awash, as in poor weather, it was nearly impossible to perform this task during a storm. The *Kineo* finally arrived in Manila in July, and Captain Patten wasted no time in expressing his disappointment with the schooner. Upon discharging her coal in Manila, the steel-hulled five-masted *Kineo* was again under sail, this time for Newcastle, Australia, to be loaded with coal for Hawaii.

With her captain cranky, her stability in an ocean gale questionable and her bottom becoming foul, the schooner headed for Newcastle on August 9, 1905. After eleven days at sea, a typhoon struck that lasted for several days. The vicious winds battered the schooner aloft; she lost her topsails, staysails, fore sails and flying jib. The high seas washed away everything on deck and contaminated the food supply. Forty-five days after leaving Manila, the *Kineo* and crew arrived in Guam, hoping to purchase fresh fruit and vegetables, as seawater had contaminated most of their stores. Unfortunately, there was none to be found, and the injured schooner again made sail.

On October 23, the first seaman became ill. The rest soon followed. The entire crew was fast stricken by a similar malady. In early December, the *Kineo* arrived in the Solomon Islands and again attempted to restore the supply of fresh fruits and vegetables. Again the crew was informed that none was available. With the crew becoming ill and supplies dangerously short—and with his wife and small daughter aboard—one wonders what Captain Frank W. Patten was thinking while his family, ship and crew languished out on the ocean on the wrong side of the world.

The *Kineo* again set sail, but after only a few days she was becalmed for over a week. Perhaps in the twenty-first century we don't have an appreciation of the word "becalmed"—"stranded" might be a better choice. Fortunately, the wind freshened and brought the *Kineo* near Cape Moreton, Australia. The steamer *Miowera* came along and brought news to Brisbane of the fate of the overdue American schooner. The entire crew was suffering from beriberi (with the exception of the captain's eight-year-old daughter). One of the crew already died from the disease.

The authorities in Brisbane removed everybody from the schooner. Nearly five weeks afterward, they had recovered and were on their way to Newcastle, Australia, to load a cargo of coal for Hawaii. After slowly discharging the coal offshore into freight lighters, over three thousand tons of sugar were loaded for a sugar refinery in Philadelphia. Still, it was not over. On the way home, trouble was found in the South Atlantic. High seas boiled and swept over the deck of the schooner, the likes of which the new crew taken on in Newcastle had never seen. To further complicate matters, the boiler failed. Now everything had to be done by hand by a crew that wasn't used to working a ship without assistance from a steam donkey engine. It had become clear that the big coasters had their limitations, and no other Down East shippers ever attempted to engage in that sort of world trade again. Eventually, two diesel engines were installed, and the *Kineo* was reduced to an oil-carrying barge. In 1916, she was sold to the Texas Company and renamed *Maryland*.

Arthur Sewall has to be credited with trying to use his schooners to work world trade routes. He was certainly a man who liked to lead and establish records. In 1892, Arthur Sewall & Company of Bath built the 311-foot-long *Roanoke*, which was the largest wooden-hulled square-rigger in the United States. The *Roanoke* was destroyed by fire in 1905. Interestingly, just a few years later in 1894, Arthur Sewall & Company built the first steel-hulled sailing vessel in the United States, a Downeaster named *Dirigo* (meaning "I lead," the motto for the state of Maine). The *Dirigo* was 312 feet long and 45 feet wide. On May 31, 1917, a German U-boat sank the *Dirigo*.

The story of the *Edna Hoyt* is the story of the last five-masted schooner ever built and the last five-masted schooner to remain in service. Built in Thomaston, Maine, by Dunn & Elliot, she was launched on December 11, 1920. In 1920, Prohibition was established, and women were given the right to vote. As if that wasn't enough, Ford's Model T was all the rage, going to the movies was becoming more and more popular, the first radio broadcast occurred, jazz was taking over and the wild and wonderful Roaring Twenties was about to commence. One might imagine that the age of commercial sail would have long since passed into the annals of not-so-recent history.

The automobile replaced the equine, and steam had nearly replaced sail, though not completely. Schooner-rigged vessels were still considered by many to be an economical way of transporting cargo. If it had to, a five-masted schooner could run with a crew of only nine men, though eleven would have been the ideal. It was the end, and not the beginning, of the *Edna Hoyt*'s career that earned her distinction. She lasted through the entire decade of the 1920s, survived the crash of '29 and was still operating as a commercial vessel on the high seas.

In 1930, she was purchased by a company out of Boston to be used primarily for the fertilizer trade between Venezuela and New England.

The *Edna Hoyt* at New York City in 1934; her deck and masts appear ghostly against the backdrop of the towering skyscrapers. *Courtesy of Maine Maritime Museum.*

Renowned New England schoonerman Captain Robert Rickson was her master. Throughout the '30s she cut many a fine dash at ports all over the world and adorned the seas with her beauty and graceful lines. She was becoming quite an attraction in her own right. In August 1934, while tied up in New York Harbor near Wall Street, her gangplank broke under the weight of overenthusiastic guests. The *Edna Hoyt* had over fifty thousand visitors that week—fifty thousand excited people who wanted to take advantage of the rare opportunity to glimpse history firsthand before it was swept off the planet and lost forever. Another incident occurred in 1935: while sitting at a dock in Portland Harbor loaded with wooden shooks (parts for assembling a barrel or box) bound for Barbados, three motion picture newsreel men waited to capture her departure from that harbor on film.

Although it might not seem so today, the '30s were, in fact, a modern era, at least relative to sailing vessels. During the decade, Birdseye frozen foods were marketed commercially, Trans World Airlines was formed as a commercial

A deck view on the five-masted *Edna Hoyt*, looking aft. *Courtesy of Maine Maritime Museum.*

airline, Ford introduced the V8 engine, the jukebox became popular and overseas telephone service was established. In the area of transportation, a land speed record of 272 miles per hour was set at Daytona Beach, and Howard Hughes flew around the world in a Lockheed aircraft in 3 days, 19 hours and 8 minutes. On the ocean front, the French vessel SS *Normandie* crossed the Atlantic in 107 hours and 33 minutes. The Maine-built schooner *Edna Hoyt* was still transporting cargo under sail and nothing else! She was one of only seventeen windjammers still working on the East Coast and the only five-masted merchant vessel afloat.

However unfortunate it seems to those of us who are hopeless romantics, we can only forestall the inevitable for so long until it manages to have its way, or else we become history ourselves. In 1937, Captain George Hopkins was master of the *Edna Hoyt* when she brought 1,650 tons of salt from Turks Island, Barbados, into Nova Scotia. She left Halifax, Nova Scotia, on September 1 with a load of one million feet of lumber to take across the

41

The pleasure of your company is requested

at the launching of the

Schooner Jennie Flood Kreger

from the yard of Mathews Brothers

Belfast, Maine

on Wednesday, March 5th, 1919

at 1 o'clock, P. M.

William R. Kreger, Master                    Crowell & Thurlow, Agents

An invitation to a launching of the five-masted Crowell & Thurlow schooner *Jennie Flood Kreger* in Belfast, Maine. *Author's collection.*

Atlantic to Ireland. It took her only twenty-two days when she had been expected to take a month. Unfortunately, time was about to overtake this graceful lady. She could escape from it no more, and soon it would strip her of her pride and sentence her to a slow and mundane existence.

The *Edna Hoyt* loaded coal in Cardiff, Wales, for Venezuela, and on November 2, 1937, she left port for that destination. In the Bay of Biscay, trouble was brewing. A terrific autumn gale punished the schooner endlessly, tossing and twisting her until one of her decks collapsed. She had thousands of tons of coal in her hold, and her weakened hull was taking on water so badly that the pumps could not keep up. She was at last defeated. On November 24, the *Hoyt* was towed into Lisbon, Portugal, by a Norwegian steamer. She was determined to be unseaworthy, and on January 14, 1938, she was purchased by Portuguese business interests, stripped of her masts and used as a floating coal barge, drawn at the end of a towline.

# The Six-Masted Giants

As the nineteenth century drew to a close in this country, the economic boom of the 1880s waned, casting a shadow over most of the following decade and including a depression. The Depression of 1893 created unemployment that exceeded 10 percent for the next several years. Banks failed, agriculture slowed, property values declined, the price of silver plummeted and the Union Pacific; Northern Pacific; and Atchison, Topeka & Santa Fe Railroads went bankrupt. In 1898, the Spanish-American War—or the "splendid little war," as Secretary of State John Hay called it—helped to turn the economy around. Wooden shipbuilding was booming again, and the demand for commercial shipping was greater than ever. The four-masted schooners worked out pretty well, and the five-masters could carry even more cargo. Would it be profitable to make a six-masted schooner? There were a few shipbuilders in Maine who thought it was worth taking a chance.

There were only ten six-masted schooners ever built, and of those nine were built in Maine. They were all built between 1900 and 1909. These massive vessels were built during the last heyday of commercial sail, and during this period they had no trouble finding work. The idea of a six-masted schooner did take getting used to, though, and there were plenty of folks who surmised that the craft would be too large and awkward to handle properly or withstand the test of time on the open sea. There was doubt that the expansive wooden hull, fully loaded with over five thousand tons of coal, could hold together without sagging or hogging. There was also some competition among the Maine shipbuilders—a race to see who could be the first to successfully build and launch one of these innovative vessels.

A six-masted
schooner in the
Mediterranean,
circa 1910.
*Author's collection.*

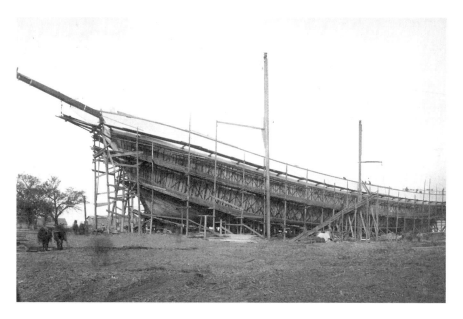

The *Wyoming* under construction at Percy & Small Shipyard in Bath, Maine. *Courtesy of Maine Maritime Museum.*

There were some businessmen in Massachusetts who wanted big schooners. John G. Crowley of Taunton, Massachusetts, the manager of the Coastwise Transportation Company, had already made lots of money with the *John B. Prescott*. The *Prescott* was a big five-masted schooner built by the Holly Bean Shipyard in Camden, Maine, in 1898. Enlisting all of his entrepreneurial insight, Mr. Crowley hired John Wardell of Rockland, Maine, to design a six-masted commercial schooner. A principal investor in this venture was the founder of the American Optical Company, Mr. George Washington Wells of Southbridge, Massachusetts.

Nearly ten thousand people waited to see the world's first six-masted schooner launched on a cloudy day in August 1900. They were watching from boats and the decks of yachts, lined up along the shore and scattered all over the shipyard. They brought their carriages and tethered their horses while they engaged in light conversation and discussed politics; they waited to see the very first six-masted schooner emerge from the New England coast. It was the *George W. Wells*, built by Holly M. Bean Shipyard and launched into the Penobscot River on August 14, 1900, in Camden, Maine. She was 342 feet long and 48 feet wide and could carry five thousand tons of cargo. The masts of this first schooner to have six were labeled as follows: fore, main, mizzen, spanker, jigger and driver. In order to be the first, the *Wells* was launched with temporary masts; the regular masts would be stepped after she was afloat.

The *Wells*'s first master, Captain Jack Crowley of Taunton, Massachusetts, was also her managing owner. She was the largest merchant vessel afloat at that time and caused quite a stir. On her maiden voyage to Havana, Cuba, with the largest load of coal ever taken to that capital, the *Wells* made the trip from Philadelphia in just over six days. On the way back from Havana, the *Wells* loaded 400,000 yellow pine railroad ties at Brunswick, Georgia, bound for New York. She made the trip in just less than four days, nearly rivaling the three days it would take a steamer to make the same run. Unfortunately, while en route from Boston to Florida in September 1913, she was lost on Diamond Shoals, Cape Hatteras, during a bitter storm. Due to the valiant efforts of the Hatteras Lifesaving Station, the fifteen crew members, three women and two children were saved. When discovered by the lifesavers, they were clinging to the schooner's rigging. The ship was a total loss.

The *Eleanor A. Percy* was launched just two months after the *Wells*, on October 10, 1900, at the Percy & Small Shipyard in Bath, Maine. She could carry over 5,500 tons of cargo and was 50 feet wide and 347 feet long overall. Although launched just two months after the *Wells*, the *Percy* was not the first, but she was certainly the largest. These Maine shipbuilders were clearly competitive and had fast become leaders in the manufacture of wooden sailing vessels, and the whole world was watching.

What an astonishing coincidence it must have been when the world's only two six-masted schooners, the *Percy* and the *Wells*, collided about 10:00 p.m. in the Atlantic Ocean during fair weather on June 29, 1901. One wonders what forces of nature contributed to this chance meeting. Whether it was

Three six-masters lie at anchor in Portland Harbor: *Addie M. Lawrence, George W. Wells* and *Eleanor A. Percy. Courtesy of Maine Maritime Museum.*

the temperament of the evening wind, the alignment of the moon and stars or just plain happenstance, the two wooden ships crashed into each other. Limping into Boston Harbor under sail, the two schooners eventually ended up at the Percy & Small Shipyard, where the costly repairs were made.

Another Percy & Small–built six-master, the *Addie M. Lawrence*, was launched on December 17, 1902, and christened with a bottle of champagne by the young lady for whom she was named. At 292 feet long and 48 feet wide, she was the smallest six-masted schooner that shipyard turned out. On August 27, 1912, the *Addie M. Lawrence* collided with Boston fishing schooner *Shenandoah* in a dense early morning fog near Nantucket, causing the *Shenandoah* to sink. The crew was rescued and taken to Vineyard Haven. Although miraculously managing to elude U-boats during World War I while carrying munitions, the *Addie M. Lawrence* went aground on the coast of France on July 9, 1917, in a gale.

It would seem that Massachusetts had to be different and launched a steel-hulled six-masted schooner. This fourth six-master was the *William L. Douglas*, and she was the only six-masted schooner that wasn't built in Maine. On August 25, 1903, she was launched at the Fore River Ship and Engine Company in Quincy, Massachusetts. This is the same company that launched the record-breaking seven-masted steel-hulled *Thomas W. Lawson* one year earlier. The *Lawson* was the largest sailing vessel ever built and was 475 feet long overall, 394 feet long on deck. She was lost in a storm off the Scilly Isles in December 1907, along with sixteen crew members.

The *William L. Douglas* was 339 feet long and 48 feet wide and could carry 5,700 tons of coal. Her six masts were steel, and her topmasts were made of Oregon pine. Unbelievably, she had a boiler that supplied the energy to run the lights, the pumps and the steering gear and heated the crew's quarters. In addition, there were four engines on her deck for hoisting the sails, raising the anchor and moving heavy cargo. But despite the boiler and the four engines, her only means of propulsion was the wind. She was equipped with twenty-two sails and nothing else. She was named after a shoe manufacturer in Brockton, Massachusetts, who was also a principal shareholder. Interestingly, Mr. Douglas was governor of Massachusetts from 1905 to 1906.

On the evening of November 6, 1909, while bound from Baltimore for Boston, the *William L. Douglas* collided with the four-masted schooner *Marguerite*, which was badly damaged. The *Douglas* struck the *Marguerite* amidships at about 11:30 p.m., the prow of the larger vessel carrying away the mainmast of the smaller. Captain Murdoch McLean of the *Douglas* went to Vineyard Haven for assistance, while the master of the *Marguerite* agreed to lie at anchor. The revenue cutter *Acushnet* was dispatched, and the disabled schooner was eventually towed to port. The six-master lost all of her headgear. In 1910, the *Douglas* was stripped of her masts and began working for the Sun Oil Company as an oil barge.

The *Ruth E. Merrill* was launched on November 23, 1904, at the Percy & Small Shipyard in Bath, Maine. She was the third six-master that shipyard would turn out and was 301 feet long and 48 feet wide. One of the most successful wooden-hulled colliers ever produced, she made record-breaking coal runs between Mid-Atlantic ports and the Northeast, specifically Portland, Maine.

On February 22, 1912, during a gale that was reported as the worst storm in years—uprooting trees, damaging houses and interrupting telegraph and telephone service—the *Merrill* washed ashore together with the barge *Ohio* at Sewall's Point near the Port of Hampton Roads, Virginia. There were ten other ships reported in distress as a result of that storm, but the six-master was not badly damaged. The *Ruth E. Merrill* would not meet her demise until January 12, 1924, when her seams opened during a severe storm, and she sank in Vineyard Sound off Massachusetts with four thousand tons of coal in her hold bound for Portland.

Another Percy & Small–built six-master was the *Alice M. Lawrence*, and she was launched on December 1, 1906. She was 305 feet long and 48 feet wide and was equipped with a steam boiler that ran the hoisting engines and pumps and provided heat and hot water for the crew. In the luxurious captain's quarters there was even a bathtub and sink with hot and cold

The horse teams at Percy & Small Shipyard in Bath, Maine. *Courtesy of Maine Maritime Museum.*

running water. The steam boiler also ran the ten-horsepower generator that furnished lighting for the ship and crew, making the *Alice M. Lawrence* the first wooden-hulled vessel to be electrified. She also carried a searchlight and was reportedly equipped with seventy-five incandescent lights.

Her first master was William Kreger of Fairfield, Maine, but eventually the *Alice M. Lawrence* ended up in the capable hands of Captain Willis B. Wormell of Portland. She was a fine vessel, and Captain Wormell often brought his family aboard. Fortunately, they weren't with him on the evening of December 5, 1914. The empty schooner was coming from Portland, Maine, and bound for Norfolk, Virginia, with her crew of thirteen, presumably to load coal. The *Lawrence* hit bad weather in Nantucket Sound, her bottom struck something on Tuckernuck Shoal, and she ran aground. As her seams began to open, the steam pumps were all that was preventing her from filling with seawater as the gale continued to batter the stranded vessel. The storm was relentless, and sixty-mile-per-hour winds thwarted efforts to rescue the ship and only drove her deeper into the shoal. The Coast Guard cutter *Acushnet* came to her assistance but was unable to save the wrecked schooner. The captain and crew remained on the *Alice M. Lawrence* until December 14, after which time she was abandoned. A year later, she was burned to the waterline.

Interestingly, on the evening of March 29, 1885, the tern schooner *French Van Gilder*, bound for Philadelphia with a load of paving stones from Somerset, Massachusetts, ran into trouble near Nantucket. She was the first schooner to lay her bones down on the Tuckernuck Shoal, her paving stones creating the hazard that ensnared the *Alice M. Lawrence*. In 1917, the Canadian coal schooner *Unique* added her bones to the pile when she grounded on what was left of the wreck of the *Alice M. Lawrence*.

The grand interior of the captain's quarters, decked out in fine style and with all of the conveniences of home. *Courtesy of Maine Maritime Museum.*

The *Mertie B. Crowley* was the largest schooner ever launched in Rockland, Maine, when she slid into the Penobscot Bay on August 24, 1907. She measured 412 feet from jib boom to spanker and 300 feet at the waterline. Her first master was Captain Emmons Babbitt. Her last master was Captain William Haskell of Boston, who also commanded the first six-master *George W. Wells*.

The *Crowley*'s brief career ended abruptly on January 23, 1910, when she wrecked on a reef three miles off Martha's Vineyard with Captain Haskell, his wife Ida and thirteen crew members aboard. The big schooner was bound from Baltimore for Boston with her hold full of coal when she was caught in a severe snowstorm. The gale was so terrific that the vessel hove to, riding out the weather for thirty hours. Anxious to deliver his cargo, as he wasn't making any profit sitting idle, Captain Haskell probably embarked for Boston too soon. When the craft finally got underway, the high seas and haze made it impossible for the helmsman to determine exactly where the ship was. At 5:30 a.m., he mistook Edgartown Light at Martha's Vineyard for Block Island Light and went aground on the shoals. Unable to endure the terrific punishment of both wave and wind, the great schooner broke in two a few hours after hitting the reef.

The story of the frightening misadventure at sea and subsequent daring rescue by the captain and crew of the small Edgartown, Massachusetts fishing smack *Priscilla* is one of the most famous tales of heroism on the North Atlantic. The *New York Times* recounts the rescue for its readers in this January 24, 1910 article entitled "10 Hours in Rigging, Saved From Wreck…Rescuers Face Wild Sea":

> *Mrs. Haskell, awakened by her husband, had barely time to snatch a few articles of clothing, and with the aid of Capt. Haskell climb into the fore rigging, where she was lashed to the crosstrees. A pair of seaman's rubber boots, with the Captain's winter hat and overcoat, protected her, and Mrs. Haskell said tonight she did not suffer greatly. All day long everybody clung to the rigging, while the seas pounded the vessel under them to fragments. At 10:00 A.M. the Crowley broke in two beneath them, and her stern settled deeper in the water. Fortunately no one was lashed at that end.*
>
> *So great was the rush of the seas that the decks were swept clear with every wave. Even the forward house was lifted off and carried away.*
>
> *Mrs. Haskell, like the others, had been lashed for ten hours to the rigging of the battered schooner. The great seas combed incessantly, over the hull and through the rigging, threatening continually to fell the masts. The fore and main mast did give way and swung wildly, but the men lashed to the trees were not dislodged and the sticks held long enough for Capt. Jackson to bring his little smack near enough to send out dories to take off the Crowley's people.*

If it wasn't for the valiant efforts and seafaring skills of Captain Levi Jackson and the fearless crew on the small fishing boat *Priscilla*, Mrs. Haskell, her husband and the thirteen crew members would surely have frozen to death or drowned in the icy below-zero maelstrom in which they were engulfed. Eyewitness accounts depict the rescuers as being covered in ice, and that ice hung everywhere and covered everything. Even the Coast Guard cutter *Acushnet*, which arrived at the scene after Captain Jackson and the *Priscilla*, stood back. It seemed that the local fisherman, who expertly worked his boat among the great breaking waves, would be the one most likely to succeed. The *New York Times* article continues:

> *By 9 o'clock this morning it was known here that a vessel had been wrecked on the northeast end reef. Efforts were made to get out to her in the forenoon, but were unsuccessful because of the great seas. The sturdy fishing smacks*

*of Edgartown could make no headway against the elements. Capt. Levi Jackson tried repeatedly to push his little power smack Priscilla through the great breakers, but combined sails and steam could not do it until late this afternoon.*

*When the Priscilla did get safely through the breakers and was anchored near the wreck four dories manned by as many stout-armed fishermen put out and were soon taking off the crew of the Crowley.*

The *Edward J. Lawrence* was launched on April 2, 1908, at the Percy & Small Shipyard in Bath, and her first master was Captain William Kreger. Over 320 feet long and 50 feet wide, the *Lawrence* was built of hard pine and oak. Perhaps her builders intuitively knew that she was to be the last six-master afloat. Managing to keep clear of reefs, rocks and other misadventures that could signal demise for a vessel, the *Lawrence* ended up sitting in Portland Harbor in the mid-1920s with the five-masted *Cora F. Cressy* and *Oakley Curtis*. The *Cressy* and the *Curtis* eventually found their way back out to sea, but the *Lawrence* remained in the harbor lying idle. In April 1925, a towboat company that claimed to have furnished steam tugs for her the year before (and received no payment) filed a suit against the vessel.

On December 27, 1925, the *Edward J. Lawrence* was destroyed by fire while sitting at anchor in Portland Harbor. Despite efforts to stop the fire in below-zero weather, a fireboat and Coast Guard cutter could not save her. The fire smoldered all night as the last six-master burned and sank in Portland Harbor. The *Lawrence* had become her own funeral pyre, turning into a ghost ship right in the harbor before everybody's eyes. Even now, at low tide near Fort Gorge's reef, it is said that some of her ribs still stick out of the muck.

The *Edward B. Winslow* was launched on November 24, 1908, at the Percy & Small Shipyard and was just over 318 feet long and 50 feet wide. She was the largest six-masted schooner in existence at the time of her launching and was built for the J.S. Winslow Company of Portland. Mr. Edward B. Winslow was a shareholder. Her first master was Captain Henry Butler of Phippsburg, Maine, and her first job was to load coal at a southern port, undoubtedly to bring back to New England.

On April 14, 1915, the steamer *Caronia*, one of the largest ships in the British Cunard Line, collided with the *Edward B. Winslow*. The *Caronia* had recently undergone conversion for use in the Royal Navy after the outbreak of World War I. The destruction was minimal, and the British admiralty agreed to pay damages. The *Edward B. Winslow* is believed to have become a casualty of World War I on July 10, 1917, when she mysteriously burned at sea with a cargo of coal within sight of the French coast. It is rumored that a German spy, under the guise of a sailor, signed on to become a crew member and planned to set fire to the ship.

The last, largest and loveliest of all the six-masters was the record-breaking *Wyoming*. Over 50 feet wide and 350 feet long on deck, 450 feet from jib boom to spanker boom, with three decks, five discharging hatches and a capacity to carry six thousand tons of coal in her hold, the *Wyoming* was the largest wooden-hulled commercial sailing vessel ever built. Carrying steam donkey hoisting engines to raise the massive sails, she was propelled only by the wind and carried thirteen thousand square yards of canvas. She was launched on December 15, 1909, at the Percy & Small yard and named after the state of Wyoming. One of her primary investors was the then governor of Wyoming, Bryant Brooks.

Interestingly, Bryant Butler Brooks was born in Hubbardston, Massachusetts, in 1861. With a love for the great outdoors, wide-open spaces

The launching of the *Wyoming* on December 15, 1909, at the Percy & Small Shipyard in Bath, Maine. *Courtesy of Maine Maritime Museum.*

and a powerful desire to become a cowboy, strong-willed B.B. Brooks ended up in Cheyenne, Wyoming, in 1880. (Wyoming became the forty-fourth state on July 10, 1890.) He hired on as a cowboy right away, worked as a trapper and a stockman and by 1883 started his own ranch. He was governor of Wyoming from 1905 to 1911.

It was Governor Brooks's daughter, Lena Natrona Brooks, who christened the *Wyoming* with a bouquet of flowers on that December afternoon in Maine. Lena was a long way from home and was a cowgirl and a pioneer in her own right. She could ride and tend the ranch just as well as any cowboy, hunted coyotes, appreciated good horses and made her life in the great expanse of Wyoming wilderness. The schooner *Wyoming* was sort of a pioneer, too—the largest of only ten six-stickers ever built—and she rode on the back of the wildest, most unforgiving bronc of all: the sea.

Captain McLeod was *Wyoming*'s first master, and he often reported that she handled like a yacht. The *Wyoming* fared well under the cautious and experienced hand of Cape Breton native Angus McLeod, perhaps with the

A view of the massive *Wyoming*, taken from the bowsprit. *Courtesy of Maine Maritime Museum.*

sole exception of her maiden voyage. By no means a disaster, the first voyage of the behemoth schooner did manage to stir anxiety in some folks. Overdue to load coal at Hampton Roads, Virginia, the vessel was also carrying young military cadet John B. Brooks, nephew of the Wyoming governor.

According to an article published in *Down East* magazine in January 1970, based on an interview of the then retired Major General John B. Brooks, young Cadet Brooks had understandably looked forward to his Christmas holiday spent away from school and to the time he would spend sailing on the great schooner. Cadet Brooks describes Captain McLeod as being conservative in the area of necessary expenditures. When the schooner left Bath, she had ten days' worth of coal, which would have been just enough to power the donkey engines and heat the cabins for the duration of the trip to the Virginia coast. Since she would be loading coal, there would doubtless be enough spilled on her deck to use to run the steam engines on the return voyage. Master McLeod saw no reason to pay for coal when he could easily have it for nothing. This philosophy would likely have worked out very well if the *Wyoming* had not been blown far off course. Twenty-one days after the oversized schooner left Bath, she finally reached Hampton Roads, Virginia. During the time they were out of coal, the crew of only thirteen had to work the huge sails by hand and suffer the cold ocean gales without the convenience of heated cabins.

The *Wyoming* had a good life as a collier, despite some lulls in shipping, working the coal routes up and down the Atlantic coast. She became a familiar figure to many, and the newspapers reported her comings and goings. She was certainly a celebrity in her last homeport of Portland. In March 1924, Captain Henry Glaesel was her master. In early March, the *Wyoming* was reported to be underway, sailing from Norfolk, Virginia, fully loaded with coal bound for New Brunswick. Another big coastal schooner was sailing along near the *Wyoming*; it was the five-masted *Cora F. Cressy*, also hailing from Portland. The *Cressy* was bound for Portland with her load of coal, and Captain Charles N. Publicover was master. On March 8, the two schooners were reported to have passed Vineyard Haven and anchored near Pollock Rip Lightship. They remained side by side for two days while a March gale stirred and battered the New England coast. Captain Publicover decided to hoist his anchors and try to get eastward, away from the coast. Both the crews on the lightship and the *Cressy* reported seeing the *Wyoming*'s lights for a while through the blowing snow. It was only the *Cora F. Cressy* that limped back to Portland. The *Wyoming* was never seen again, although pieces of her washed ashore a few days later. She was lost with all hands.

# The Celebrated
## Governor Ames

The history of both Maine and Massachusetts are inextricably linked. For many years during the early colonization of what is now known as New England, Maine was considered to be a part of Massachusetts. In 1691, William and Mary, joint rulers of the Kingdom of England, chartered the Province of Massachusetts Bay. Included in this vast tract of land was the Plymouth Colony, the Province of Maine, the islands of Martha's Vineyard and Nantucket and also, unbelievably, what is now known as Nova Scotia. Maine finally gained independence from Massachusetts on March 15, 1820, when it became the twenty-third state in the Union. Often, however, it was the interchange of talent from both locales that brought about the realization of a common goal.

The history of some of the most famous Maine schooners and the history of the town of Somerset, Massachusetts, are strangely connected. Without knowledge of both, neither history would be complete. There are two different stories that link the histories together. The first, in 1888, is the story of the Maine-built schooner *Governor Ames*, the first five-masted oceangoing vessel ever constructed on the East Coast, as well as the Massachusetts man from Somerset who made it happen.

I knew that if I were to do justice to the story I would need to visit the town of Somerset, get a whiff of some of the salt in the air and look out over the Taunton River where the ships would invariably have sat at anchor back in that era—back during a time when the air was fresh and crisp, the clouds billowed as white as the sails and there were no streams of corrupting black smoke rising upward to infiltrate the heavens.

Pulling into the parking lot of the old brick school building that housed the Somerset Historical Society, I could not help but notice the sign in front of the building. It unmistakably depicted a Maine five-masted schooner under full sail. I could have parked anywhere, but I turned to the left and stopped my vehicle, settling for a nice spot overlooking the Taunton River. I sat for a moment taking in the view; then I opened the door and slid down onto the running board and out of my truck. I noticed, as soon as my boots hit the earth, that there was a special quality about the place. There was something quietly stirring in the air, sort of a slow rambling momentum in cadence with the river itself.

I surveyed what lay before me: there was a knoll overlooking the waterfront, and strategically placed on that was a striking Georgian home with two chimneys at each end and a prominent widow's walk situated above the center of the roof. It surely had the look of a sea captain's home if ever there was one. I continued to stare at the magnificent residence.

"That's the Henry Bowers House," explained Diane Goodwin, president of the Somerset Historical Society.

> *His father, Jonathan, built the first commercial shipyard here in 1695. It's an interesting house, too, because Captain John Burgess owned it. He was the famous captain of the clipper ship* David Crockett *and had quite a reputation as a tough master. In April 1874, his crew mutinied after they were cleared to leave San Francisco for Liverpool with a cargo of wheat, and later during that same voyage he was washed overboard during a storm off South America. Have you heard of the song "The Leaving of Liverpool"? The song is about Captain Burgess and the* David Crockett.

"This is certainly quite an interesting place," I replied. "I cannot wait to learn more about Captain Cornelius Davis."

"His father, Captain Nathan Davis, had five sons, and they all became sea captains. You'll find we have a very rich seafaring history in Somerset."

It soon became very clear how a man from this place could make maritime history. The folks of Somerset lived and breathed the sea and built and sailed the ships. Innovative and inspired, they built clippers, brigs, whaling barks, sloops and schooners and plied the seas in any way they could.

Incorporated in 1790, Somerset was named for Somerset Square in Boston, which was named for Somerset, England. Formerly a part of Swansea, Massachusetts, the Wampanoag people knew Somerset as the land of "Shawomet." It was known later as the Shawomet Purchase when the Court of Plymouth ordered its sale in 1677 to relieve debt created by King

Philip's War. The area was settled shortly afterward. Located on the Taunton River and bordering Mount Hope Bay and Narragansett Bay; just east of Providence, Rhode Island; and south of Boston, Somerset was naturally placed for commerce by the sea. Additionally, proximity to developing communities such as Fall River and New Bedford was strategic as well.

Somerset became known for its seafarers and its seafaring families. The son of Captain Jonathan Davis, Captain Nathan Davis was the father of five sons who also became sea captains. Captain Nathan "Deacon" Davis of Somerset was a staunch believer that consuming alcoholic spirits brought about ruination, and he practiced what he preached. As a young man, he assisted in the construction of his own sloop, *Temperance*, banned the consumption of liquor throughout the entire process and then christened the ship with a bottle of water instead of rum. Of course, liquor was never drunk aboard the *Temperance*.

Sometimes it seems that people are shaped both by the land that rears them and the blood that flows through their veins. The sons of Captain Nathan "Deacon" Davis were determined. They were also of the sea, and their stories are worth mentioning. Captain Elijah "Danger" Davis was born in Somerset in 1832. In 1865, he was captured by the Confederates and sent to the infamous Libby Prison in Richmond, Virginia, for transporting supplies in his schooner *Lucy Robinson* to Union soldiers during the Civil

A seafarer's home and family: the residence of Captain Nathan Davis. *Courtesy of Somerset Historical Society.*

War. He survived to become a commodore with the Fall River Steamship Line along with his older brother Nathan. Unfortunately, younger brother Captain Amos Davis was lost at sea.

In 1872, it was the opening of the Old Colony Railroad that led to the establishment of Somerset as a major coal port. It was the need for large colliers that spurred on the development of the first big coastal schooners near the end of the nineteenth century. Captain Joseph Davis was born in Somerset in 1839 and his younger brother Captain Cornelius Davis, in 1847. The two brothers went into the coal business and formed the Atlantic Shipping Company.

In 1888, the Davis brothers, the Atlantic Shipping Company, a ship designer named Albert Winslow from nearby Taunton, Massachusetts, and a shipbuilder from Waldoborough, Maine, combined their efforts. Captain Cornelius Davis commissioned Albert Winslow to design a large four-masted schooner for the coal and overseas trade. Mr. Winslow created the customary wooden three-dimensional half model of the hull, but further scrutiny revealed, in his opinion, the need for a fifth mast. The product that arose from a culmination of efforts by an entrepreneurial sea captain from Somerset, a ship-designing genius from Taunton and a damn good Maine shipbuilder was an event that made maritime history. It was the launching of the first five-masted oceangoing schooner on the East Coast.

The *Governor Ames* was launched into the Medomak River from the Leverett Storer Shipyard in Waldoborough, Maine, on December 1, 1888. There was some rushing to get her launched, as the Medomak River usually freezes in December, making navigation impossible. Built for the Atlantic Shipping Company in Somerset, this revolutionary schooner was named after the then governor of Massachusetts, Oliver Ames, who was an investor. The *Governor Ames* was an impressive 265 feet long and nearly 50 feet wide and could carry three thousand tons of coal. The crew's quarters, or fo'c'sle, were located below decks forward, and the captain's quarters were finished in polished oak. There were also spare staterooms and cabins aft.

Incorporating the latest in technology, she carried a thirty-horsepower steam engine for hoisting sails and anchors. The five masts were thirty inches in diameter and 115 feet long, in addition to the 56-foot topmasts. The *Ames* carried seven thousand square yards of sail. The official name on the ship was *Gov. Ames*, the abbreviated form supposedly being less expensive for telegraph purposes, and her homeport was Providence, Rhode Island.

The *Ames* slid down the ways at eight o'clock in the morning, and it must have been pretty cold, but despite this there were plenty of folks who came

Captain Cornelius Davis of
Somerset, Massachusetts, first master
and part owner of the *Governor Ames*.
*Courtesy of Maine Maritime Museum.*

to see the historic launching of the mammoth schooner. There were even extra cars attached to the regular freight train just to accommodate the anticipated spectators.

Often touted as being the first five-masted schooner in the world, or at least the first oceangoing five-masted schooner, the *Governor Ames* is really neither. She was the first five-masted schooner ever built on the East Coast, though, and certainly the most famous early five-masted schooner. In 1883, the *David Dows* was the first five-masted schooner ever built, and she was intended for the Great Lakes trade. The Oregon-built five-masted schooner *Louis* was built in October 1888 but did not have the tonnage of the *Ames*.

Both Cornelius and Joseph Davis were on board when the schooner left Waldoborough on her maiden voyage. Captain Cornelius Davis was in command, while Captain Joseph Davis was along for the ride to see how the innovative new craft handled. Unfortunately, the *Ames*'s first voyage was beset with difficulty.

On Sunday, December 9, 1888, she sailed from Waldoborough in ballast for Baltimore, Maryland. Everything went along well, and the brothers were pleased with the way the ship handled and the speed she could maintain. After

Captain Joseph Davis of Somerset, Massachusetts. *Courtesy of Somerset Historical Society.*

a few days, however, they were met with unrelenting gale-force winds that caused a splice in one of the schooner's head stays to break. Losing support from the rigging, the foremast fell first, taking all of the other masts with it. The huge masts fell into the ocean, one after the other, but miraculously nobody was injured. Still tethered by rigging, the masts bumped the *Ames*'s hull as she drifted helplessly. Unable to navigate, the dismasted schooner was blown up onto the rocky ledge of Georges Bank and stranded. There they remained for several days until the fishing schooner *Ethel Maude* of Gloucester found them.

Captain Joseph Davis made a bargain with the master, and the *Ethel Maude* brought him back to Gloucester, where he found a train to Boston. It was there that he was able to arrange for a rescue and tow for the damaged schooner. Luckily, the crew members remaining aboard had enough food and water. The captain of the nearby revenue cutter *Albert Gallatin* refused to take his ship out in the storm, but Joseph Davis would not give up. He finally managed to enlist the assistance of the largest steam tug in the world, the *H.F. Morse*, and the *Governor Ames* finally made it back into Boston for repairs. The following is an account given by Captain Joseph Davis to a *New York Times* correspondent on December 17, 1888, after he was brought ashore by the Gloucester fishing schooner:

> *My brother and myself were well pleased at the way the vessel behaved, as she gave evidence of being speedy and a good sea boat. Tuesday morning*

*the wind breezed up from the southwest and increased to a hurricane. The standing rigging became slack, and in spite of the fact that we kept setting it up the foremast went by the board about 9 o'clock Tuesday night. In falling the foremast carried with it main, mizzen, and juggermasts, leaving the schooner entirely dismasted and unmanageable. We anchored, paying out 180 fathoms of chain, and proceeded to clear away the wreck. The wire standing rigging was piled up all over the hull, and the spars alongside were pounding the vessel. The standing rigging holding the wreckage was severed and the masts sent adrift. Two of them, the main and mizzen that had parted near the splice below deck were secured. Two of the others kept company with us for 48 hours. To add to our difficulty the cable parted, and we began to drift, bringing up at last on the rocky bottom of Georges. Here we remained clearing up and waiting for assistance. Up to Sunday we saw but few vessels, and they passed us at a distance. Sunday the fishing schooner Ethel Maude of Gloucester ran down to us, and we made a bargain for a passage for myself and two extra carpenters to Gloucester. I left the Governor Ames at 6 o'clock Sunday night in latitude 41° 15' north, longitude 67° 40' west, and arrived in Boston via Gloucester to-day.*

For a short time, the idea of putting five masts on a schooner didn't seem like a good one to lots of folks, and the schooner would now have to prove herself. By mid-February 1889, the *Ames* was ready to sail again. Her masts were shortened and more adequately secured, and she again became pleasing to the eye. She was due to leave Boston for Portland, Maine, to pick up nearly two million feet of spruce and pine, to be delivered to Buenos Aires. This was one of the largest lumber cargoes even taken by an American vessel. The *Ames* left for South America on April 30, arriving there in just over two months. Over the next year, she carried coal from Mid-Atlantic ports into New England and even brought ice from Boothbay, Maine, into Philadelphia during one return trip in the summer of 1890.

In the fall of 1890, the coal freights waned considerably, and the *Ames* still hadn't paid for herself (or even paid a dividend to her investors). The culprit was the costly repair incurred by the dismasting on her maiden voyage. Something had to be done, and Cornelius Davis wasted no time. Courageous, determined and confident in his vessel, the innovative captain decided to make history once more. He would sail his large schooner through the treacherous seas around the tip of Cape Horn and capitalize on the more lucrative shipping opportunities that existed on the West Coast at that time.

The *Governor Ames* at Puget Sound, with Captain Cornelius Davis's two daughters, Alma and Clara, on deck. Each child is holding a doll, and they are accompanied by their dog. Closer scrutiny reveals a face in the window behind the girls; perhaps it is their mother. *Courtesy of Maine Maritime Museum.*

Since fore- and aft-rigged ships were notoriously difficult to handle in heavy seas—rolling and pitching due to their lack of stabilizing square sails—taking such a large schooner through those waters was certainly a daring feat. Unbelievably, it was not uncommon for a shipmaster to bring his wife and family along on a voyage. Cornelius Davis must have had tremendous faith in his vessel because he took his family with him on the journey to the West Coast, including his two little girls, Alma and Clara.

In September 1890, the *Ames* was dry-docked in Baltimore so that her bottom could be scraped and coppered in preparation for the westward journey. Afterward, she loaded just over two thousand tons of coal for delivery to the port of San Francisco and was underway on October 25. The *Governor Ames* became the first five-masted schooner ever to round Cape Horn, and she was the only one to do it successfully, although her captain did state afterward that the ship rolled badly during the storms. She sailed twice around the Horn and for four years was engaged in transporting coal along the West Coast and carrying lumber to Australia from Pacific ports. The *Ames* also brought coal to Hawaii, where Captain Davis and his family remained for one month before heading to Puget Sound to load lumber for Redondo, California. Next, she loaded lumber at Port Blakely, Washington, bound for Liverpool. After a lengthy absence of four years, Captain Cornelius Davis would finally be able to head back to his home in Somerset after discharging his cargo of lumber in England.

# From Glory Days to Ghost Ships

In August 1894, the *Governor Ames* was again working the coastal coal trade on the East Coast. Back and forth she went between Newport News, Virginia, and Providence, Rhode Island, satisfying New England's growing appetite for coal. Then, on February 5, 1895, the *Governor Ames* left Salem, Massachusetts, with her master Captain Davis and a crew of twelve bound for Philadelphia. She was noted to have passed Highland Light near Cape Cod on the same day. Not long afterward, a tremendous northwest gale struck the ship and pushed her eastward, farther away from her destination. Snow and hail punished the schooner and the men for several more days until a hurricane struck, blowing the mainsail away. It was the only sail that had been set. The force of the wind was so great that it pushed the schooner into the sea and covered her deck with five feet of water.

After fourteen days, the vessel was still being blown farther off course, and Captain Davis tried to sail to the south to get around the storm, but his efforts were for naught. On the seventeenth day and still trying to get to Philadelphia, the massive five-master approached Bermuda instead. By this time, the *Governor Ames* was reported as "missing" by many newspapers on the East Coast, and the public waited hopefully for her return. The *Ames* had been blown 750 miles southeast of her destination, and unfortunately the next port she was able to make was Norfolk, Virginia, and that wasn't until March 5. Exactly one month after leaving Salem, Massachusetts, the *Governor Ames* sailed into the Virginia harbor as the steamers blew their whistles to celebrate the return of the long-awaited sailing vessel. It was 1895, nearly the twentieth century, and everybody knew that the end of an age was soon to come.

The *Governor Ames* with all sails set. There are two men in the rigging near the stern. *Courtesy of Maine Maritime Museum.*

Cornelius Davis retired from the sea sometime about 1896, and the *Governor Ames* saw a new master, Captain G.W. Waldman, who brought her through many successful coal runs and other voyages. The *Ames* wasn't always the ship in need of assistance when ocean storms were howling and blowing, and it wasn't always steamers that came to the aid of sailing vessels.

On January 25, 1898, the *New York Times* reported that a small two-masted steamer, the *Tillie*, was abandoned at sea off Barnegat, New Jersey, and that the vessel was loaded with guns and dynamite intended for the "warring Cubans." It is important to note that things were getting hot in Cuba about this time, and the USS *Maine* had only just arrived in Havana that day. The subsequent sinking of the *Maine* in that harbor less than one month afterward, killing 266 men, was the event that helped to bring about the Spanish-American War. The paper also reports that the coasting schooner *Governor Ames* rescued nineteen people from the steamer.

Captain Waldman noticed the steamer flying her flag union down, a signal of distress. Although in the midst of a raging storm, with winds over forty miles per hour, the seas high and water washing over the deck of the *Ames*, the overworked crew members of the schooner did their best to save the people aboard the sinking steamer. Carefully maneuvering their ship the best they could in the storm, the *Ames* crew threw ropes over the side of their vessel and hauled the steamer's survivors aboard their wooden-hulled sailing craft. Four men could not be saved, as the seas and the nighttime finally overcame the valiant rescue effort, but the *Ames* did take nineteen survivors into Providence.

On May 30, 1899, bound for Galveston, Texas, from Philadelphia with coal, the *Governor Ames* came ashore thirty-eight miles from Key West in only eighteen feet of water. She was refloated the following day after two hundred tons of coal in her hold had been removed. The vessel was unscathed and continued her career, undoubtedly enjoying the more favorable freight opportunities of the early part of the next century.

After 1902, Captain Albert M. King from Lunenberg, Nova Scotia, became her final master. The *Ames* took coal to southern ports and often returned with railroad ties from Brunswick, Georgia. In early December 1909, the *Governor Ames* left Brunswick heavily laden with thirty-three thousand railroad ties bound for New York. Instead, during a gale on December 13 at approximately 11:30 a.m., she was blown onto Wimble Shoals, twenty-five miles north of Cape Hatteras, North Carolina. The ties were in her hold and piled high on her deck.

The ship filled with water as her stern began to break up, shuddering and creaking and working her way deeper into the sand. The seas washed

The *Governor Ames* waits at a dock in Galveston, Texas. *Courtesy of Maine Maritime Museum.*

over the deck, setting the railroad ties adrift to crash into crew members and wreak further havoc on the vessel. Mrs. King, the master's wife who was also aboard, was wrapped in a blanket and lashed to the rigging, as that was thought to be the safest place. At about 2:30 p.m., the hull broke in two, and then the spanker and mizzenmasts fell onto the deck and into the seas. The helpless crew tried vainly to manufacture a raft out of the railroad ties. After a few more hours, the mainmast fell, crushing Mrs. King and some others on deck. The remaining crew members were maimed and then drowned with the exception of one man, who managed to get away from the dangerous wreck by clinging all night to a floating hatch. This sole survivor was Josiah Spearing, a sailor from Nova Scotia. The following morning, the watch officer on the steamer *Shawmut*, which was en route to Charleston, saw the floating wreckage and picked up the sailor. Clad in his dripping oilskin, cut and bruised from his ordeal on the schooner and chilled from the icy waters, Mr. Spearing told the frightful account of the last day of the first great five-master.

It may be interesting to note that the steamer's name was *Shawmut*. The *Ames* was a ship whose beginnings were conceived in the town of Somerset, formerly known as Shawomet. "Shawmut" and "Shawomet" are different spellings for a Wampanoag word meaning the same thing, usually referring to either a saltwater landing or ending place.

Over 120 years have passed since the great schooner *Governor Ames* slid down the ways in Waldoborough, Maine, making maritime history, and just over 100 years since she ran aground and was wrecked on the sandy shoals of North Carolina, passing into oblivion. Most folks today have no knowledge of her existence or of the story of the coastal schooners that helped to forestall the end of an age.

Now it is the twenty-first century, and the era of the commercial sailing vessel has passed, along with that of the horse and carriage, never again to return. Nevermore will we see or experience the merchant vessel out on the ocean with all sails set, as she has sailed into that inescapable void where what is becomes what was and passes into history.

The people of Somerset haven't forgotten their history, though, or the story of the first five-masted schooner. Somerset keeps its past close by, and in 2008, 120 years after its launching, the *Governor Ames* was still remembered by the townspeople. Invited to participate in a celebration of maritime history, citizens made their marks on a canvas commemorating the *Governor Ames* during the "Spirit of Somerset Festival." In the tradition of pointillism, each person left a colored point of ink, which was incorporated into a mosaic that formed a portrait of the great ship, proudly riding the sea with all sails set. The painting is currently hanging in the Somerset Public Library.

# A Five-Masted
# Ghost Ship

## *The* Carroll A. Deering

What is a "ghost ship"? The definition seems to be as elusive as the thing itself. Who hasn't been intrigued by stories of mysterious ships such as the *Mary Celeste* or the *Flying Dutchman*? Why do these tales of unexplained phenomena stir us so and rouse our imaginations, even if we have never ventured near the sea? One cannot help but wonder how these things come to pass and what it is that forever taints a vessel with such foreboding that it is always envisioned against the backdrop of dark clouds or dense fog. What really makes a ship into a ghost ship?

The five-masted Maine-built schooner *Carroll A. Deering* was launched in 1919. She was distinguished in many ways. The first, and least exciting, is her distinction of being the schooner whose name was most frequently misspelled. Also, she was the largest, loveliest and last vessel built by the G.G. Deering Company of Bath, Maine. She was the ninety-ninth ship the then eighty-six-year-old Gardiner G. Deering had built, and she was the pinnacle of his career—the finest lady ever crafted by this man who lived just to build ships. She was breathtakingly beautiful and grand—certainly the sort of ship one could not help but take note of, the kind that commands attention and compels us to stare, that sort of a ship. The day of the sailing vessel might have been waning, but "Gard" Deering certainly wasn't going to let that stop him or the *Carroll A. Deering*. The fact that she was launched nearly twenty years into the twentieth century, long after most of her kind of wooden sailing vessel had vanished, is in itself remarkable. But even that pales compared to what had lay ahead for her.

The launching of the handsome *Carroll A. Deering* on April 4, 1919. Less than two years later, she will take her place in history as a "ghost ship." *Courtesy of Maine Maritime Museum.*

Gardiner G. Deering of Bath, Maine, builder of the *Carroll A. Deering* and ninety-eight other ships. *Courtesy of Maine Maritime Museum.*

The *Carroll A. Deering*, named after the shipbuilder's youngest son, was launched into the Kennebec River on April 4, 1919, nearly one hundred years after the first ocean crossing of an American steam-propelled vessel. She had nothing to propel her but the wind and carried six thousand yards of sail. A steam-powered donkey engine would make easy work of hoisting her sails. She was 255 feet long and 44 feet wide and weighed 2,114 tons. Her masts were 108 feet tall, and in addition her topmasts were 46 feet

Mariners discuss business in an aft cabin. They have tossed their hats onto a nearby chair and are enjoying cigars while embroiled in conversation. *Courtesy of Maine Maritime Museum.*

tall. Built primarily to be a collier, she could carry more than 3,500 tons of coal, and she had three decks. She was the largest ship the G.G. Deering Company in Bath had ever turned out.

William M. Merritt of Portland, Maine, became her master, as well as a shareholder. Captain Merritt was well known as a schoonerman, and it was he who was master of the five-masted schooner *Dorothy B. Barrett* when a German U-boat sunk her in 1918. Now he had a nice new boat, and the Great War was over. The *Carroll A. Deering* became lucrative immediately, carrying Pennsylvania and West Virginia coal from Newport News, Virginia, to Brazil, Spain and Puerto Rico. She also brought coal back to her homeport and the rest of New England in the coastwise trade. For a wooden-hulled, wind-powered sailing vessel in the early twentieth century, the *Carroll A. Deering* was doing quite well and making a good profit besides.

It wasn't until September 1920 that things began to take a calamitous turn. The first event in the downward spiral was the sudden illness that befell Captain Merritt. He became so ill, in fact, that he had to check into a hotel in Delaware, hoping to shake his illness, while his five-masted schooner lay idle and anchored, fully laden with coal bound for Rio de Janeiro.

Time was money, and with Bill Merritt sick in bed, the clock was ticking. It soon became apparent that a replacement had to be found, and Captain Merritt suggested that his friend and neighbor, Willis Wormell, take over as temporary master of the *Deering*. Captain Willis B. Wormell was a renowned schoonerman himself and former master of the enormous six-masted *Alice M. Lawrence*. However, at sixty-six years of age, Mr. Wormell was enjoying his retirement with his family in Portland and was probably trying to put his career behind him. Still, it must have bewitched him, tempted him and called to him whenever he looked out into the harbor and saw the horizon meet the sea.

When the call for help from the Deering Company came, Captain Wormell wasted no time, and within days he was in the salt water and en route to Rio via his preferred mode of transportation, a big Down East schooner, and a handsome one at that. How he must have felt alive again when he boarded the familiar craft and walked on her deck, as might a child who had just found a favorite toy that had been lost. Willis Wormell was once again Captain Wormell.

The *Deering* arrived in the port of Rio de Janeiro in late November, and her coal was discharged via the slow hand-shoveling method by overworked Brazilian dockworkers. The whole process went along much more quickly in the states, where the gantry cranes on the dock made a much easier job of discharging heavy cargo. Yet the captain had no complaint about the amount of time that it took to discharge his cargo; that was to be expected, but he did have another complaint. He complained about his mostly Scandinavian crew and especially his Scotch mate. The schooner had a crew of ten besides the captain, and the only man he was comfortable with was the engineer from Maine who ran the steam hoisting engine.

Coincidentally, another schooner built in Bath, Maine, was laid up at the same wharf in Rio. The five-masted *Governor Brooks* was there for repairs, and her master, George Goodwin, also hailed from Maine. It was to Captain Goodwin that Captain Wormell complained. It was becoming increasingly difficult to obtain good crews for sailing vessels; most men chose to work on steamers, where the pay and the accommodations were considered preferable. They also knew exactly when they would arrive at their destination. They didn't have to wait for the irresolute wind. It was the twentieth century after all.

The *Governor Brooks* was built by the Percy & Small Shipyard, practically next door to G.G. Deering Company, and was launched in April 1907. However, due to the limited shipbuilding ways at the Percy & Small Shipyard at that time, the ship was actually built on adjoining property owned by the G.G. Deering Company. It is interesting that these two five-masted schooners built in Bath were lying so close to each other at the docks in Rio at the same time in 1920. It is quite ironic, because neither one of them ever made it back to her homeport. After the *Governor Brooks* finally departed Rio in March 1921, she took on water during a storm and was sunk off Montevideo, Uruguay. There was another graceful lady gone. The crew was rescued by a passing British steamer. What was left of the ship was torched to prevent it from becoming a navigation hazard.

The *Deering*, with her less-than-desirable crew and an uncomfortable Captain Wormell, left Rio on December 2, 1920, bound for Barbados, where things would only get worse. It would seem that the rum in Barbados was too much of a temptation for the first mate, and the rest of the crew didn't need much coaxing to join in. The result was a drunken rampage that went on for several days, ending only when the first mate was arrested and incarcerated for disorderly conduct. Sometime during this unfortunate course of events, witnesses heard the mate threaten to kill the captain. Despite this behavior, however, Captain Wormell bailed him out of jail and took him back aboard ship, likely hoping that their voyage would be over soon.

One can only imagine how many times this decent, god-fearing family man from Maine wished that he had never agreed to become master of this schooner with this crew. The *Carroll A. Deering* was lovely, she was graceful and she rode the seas as well as any fine schooner. The captain's quarters were finished with imported woods and fit for royalty. Everything on the ship was solid and seaworthy, and everything about the *Carroll A. Deering* inspired confidence, except for the crew.

The *Deering* left Barbados on January 9, 1921, bound for Hampton Roads, Virginia. Captain Willis B. Wormell from Portland, Maine, was never seen again. There was a storm brewing somewhere along the North Carolina coast. On January 29, 1921, at 4:30 p.m., Lookout Shoals Light Vessel 80 reported a five-masted schooner passing with all sails set, riding high in the sea, clearly without a cargo. She was so remarkable a sight that the lightship's engineer photographed her as she passed close by. It was 1921, after all, and sailing ships were soon becoming a thing of the past. A sailor on her deck hailed the lightship, stating that the schooner had lost her anchors in the gale and to notify the owners. It was noted the sailor had an accent and was thought to be Scandinavian. It was also noted that the other sailors were apparently lounging about near the captain's quarters, where they should not have been. There was no sign of the captain.

Soon after the schooner passed, a steamer was seen approaching the lightship from the same direction. Enthusiastic to get a message to the owners of the schooner about the loss of her anchors, and with their own wireless not working, the captain of the lightship hailed the steamer, but she did not reply. He then blew the steam whistle to alert the steamer of the need to stop, but this only resulted in the ship changing course, speeding up and steering away from the lightship while crew members rushed to cover the ship's nameplate with a canvas. Was the steamer hijacked by Russian spies? Was she a rumrunner carrying a cargo of bootleg liquor?

In January 1921, there was a cargo much more lucrative than coal, and Barbados was dripping with it. Nearly one year earlier, on January 16, 1920, the National Prohibition Act went into effect. In 1919, the Eighteenth Amendment, which prohibited the sale and manufacture of "intoxicating liquor," was ratified but wasn't enforced. Despite President Woodrow Wilson's veto, the Volstead Act, which established a definition of "intoxicating liquor," was passed, and by January 1920 the United States was dry. This "Noble Experiment" was the culmination of years of protest by the Women's Christian Temperance Union and others to remove the evils of alcohol from society.

Although a comic figure by today's standards, axe-wielding and Bible-clutching spokeswoman for the WCTU Carry A. Nation certainly got her point across as she traveled about the country smashing bottles of booze in saloons and barrooms. Blaming her alcoholic first husband for the destruction of their marriage, Carry A. Nation went one step further and eventually identified liquor as the culprit in the ruination of all society. Despite her sudden death in 1911 after she collapsed following a lengthy discourse on the evils of spirits, the country was still feeling the effects of her scorn in January 1921—even, quite possibly, in an anchorless schooner sailed by an unsavory crew that was headed for the North Carolina coast.

There is something that happens when darkness encroaches on daytime and spawns night. The tangible business of the day fades and begins to lose its definition, and it becomes harder and harder to tell where a thing begins and where it ends. Barriers are broken, borders are breached and the soul of a thing can change. What was once known becomes at best surreal. But what the break of dawn revealed on the morning of January 31, 1921, near Cape Hatteras, North Carolina, is a matter of record; it is fact. There was something out on the shoals, just within sight of the U.S. Coast Guard station. There was something barely discernable through the rain, crashing seas and rising mist. There was a great five-masted schooner with all sails set, listing slightly starboard and sitting right up on the bank. Her beautiful white hull had turned gray. The change had come sometime in the night; the *Carroll A. Deering* was now a ghost ship. A ghost ship you could see, one whose creaking timbers could be heard and one you could touch, but it was a ghost ship nonetheless.

It was several days before the sea settled down enough for the Coast Guard cutters to get close. When they finally did get near, they were able to see her name and homeport and that there seemed to be nobody aboard. They also noted that the yawl boat was missing. Did the crew flee from the schooner in the midst of the storm and meet their demise in the sea? There were no bodies or wreckage about. Was the great ship deliberately run aground? Was she abandoned at sea? Except for the flying jib, all sails were set, and the relentless wind had driven her deep into the sand. She was finished.

When the Coast Guard boarded the vessel, there was no sign of life at all, except for three ship's cats. The forecastle was barren, the ship's instruments and log were missing and the captain's quarters were in disarray. The ocean chart was spread out on a table, and somebody had been making notations. There was still a pot of pea soup and a pan with spare ribs in the galley, as well as a pot of coffee on the stove. The *Carroll A. Deering* had certainly become a ghost ship.

The sulfur steamship *Hewitt* was lost the same night that the *Deering* ran aground. The *Hewitt* was bound for Portland, Maine, and was on a course similar to the *Deering*. One theory speculates that the steamship rescued the schooner's crew, only to be lost herself shortly afterward. No trace of the *Hewitt* was ever found.

There were many theories to explain what was happening to the seemingly growing number of ships that had gone missing in the same area. Long before the "Bermuda Triangle" hypothesis became popular, many speculated that the ships had fallen prey to the rumrunning criminal element. Just two years after the end of the Great War, others believed that the ships hit leftover floating mines or were the victims of a renegade German U-boat captain who was still fighting the war. With the fear of Communism rampant, there was even speculation that Russian pirates were subduing ship's crews and bringing the boats back to Russia for the Bolsheviks.

Back in Portland, Maine, the Wormell family had difficulty accepting their tragic loss, and daughter Lula must have lain awake at night searching for reasons to believe that her father might still be alive. Accepting the loss became even more difficult when, in the spring, a North Carolina fisherman claimed to have found a message in a bottle that had washed up on shore.

The note inside, he said, was written by the engineer of the *Carroll A. Deering* who hailed from Maine. Written on the small piece of paper stuffed into the bottle was a message that noted that the crew had been captured by pirates in an oil-burning boat.

It was May 1921, and Lula Wormell still wanted to find her missing father, who she now supposed had been captured by Russian pirates. The bottle message was sent to Maine and inspected by handwriting experts to determine its authenticity. When a Maine senator became involved, the whole affair gained the momentum it needed to become a national investigation, and Lula Wormell boarded a train in Portland that would get her to Washington, D.C. Folks likely wondered if all girls from Maine had the moxie of Miss Wormell.

Newly elected president Warren G. Harding had recently appointed supporter Herbert Hoover as secretary of commerce. Hoover was anxious to earn a good reputation in his new job and gain popularity besides. Hoover wanted good public relations; he wanted to eventually become president himself. The mysteriously grounded five-masted schooner from Maine was causing quite a stir in the newspapers and in general conversation. When Lula Wormell asked the secretary of commerce to use the U.S. Navy and any other resource at his disposal to find her missing father, Mr. Hoover was only too happy to consent. This man, who would be elected thirty-first president of the United States and take office in 1929, only months before the stock market crashed, promised Miss Lula Wormell that he would find her missing father. He also promised a nation, in his campaign slogan for 1928, that he would put "a chicken in every pot and a car in every garage" if he were elected president. Unfortunately, despite his best efforts, Mr. Hoover was able to do neither.

In late August 1921, the bottle message was found to be a hoax. The fisherman who discovered it, when pressured by Hoover's special assistant Lawrence Richey, admitted that it was a fake. Despite all of Herbert Hoover's efforts, no government agency, including the U.S. Navy, was ever able to find the master of the schooner from Maine or any information pertaining to the incident at all.

The bones of what was left of the *Carroll A. Deering*, after she was mercilessly beaten and broken by wind and sea, eventually washed up on the North Carolina shore. At some point, the part of her hull that held the capstan was hauled away from its resting place and dragged to a local gas station for display.

# Twentieth-century Pirates

## The Dreaded U-boats

They were often called "raiders" and much, much worse. Teddy Roosevelt called them pirates, but they were actually German submarines trying to cut the supply lines between America and Britain during World War I. Submarines weren't very sophisticated about 1914, and it was found that they were best suited as raiders of merchant vessels, used in an attempt to create a blockade around the British Isles. The term "U-boat" was just an abbreviation of the German *Unterseeboot*, meaning undersea boat. The longer the war dragged on, the more desperately Germany needed to cut England off from the rest of the world. The role of the U-boat was simple: attack and sink any merchant vessels that might be delivering supplies to Great Britain or its allies. These attacks were not very well received by the United States or the rest of the world.

In 1915, after a U-boat sank the British liner RMS *Lusitania*, with over one hundred American lives lost, President Wilson demanded an end to attacks on passenger ships, but by February 1917 the Germans had resumed unrestricted submarine warfare. By April 1917, after German U-boats had sunk numerous U.S. merchant ships and a German plot to bring Mexico into the war was uncovered, the United States entered the Great War.

In 1918, growing more desperate to prevent goods from reaching Britain, Germany began converting its large merchant submarines into ships of war. These huge, long-range submarines were classified as type U-151 boats or U-cruisers, specifically designed to take the war to the U.S. coast. This was a time when there were many large schooners engaged in the coasting trade, as well as crossing the Atlantic. Since windjammers were notoriously slow and difficult to maneuver, they became perfect targets.

The five-masted *Dorothy B. Barrett* plunges into oblivion in the Atlantic as she succumbs to a U-boat attack on August 14, 1918. *Courtesy of Maine Maritime Museum.*

The very first U-151 boat was actually called *U-151*, and she arrived in the Atlantic coast in May 1918. At first, she laid mines near Delaware and also cut submerged telegraph cables; then on May 25 she stopped three schooners off the Virginia coast. The crews were taken prisoner to prevent them from warning other vessels, and their schooners were sunk. One must give the *U-151* commander, Korvetten-Kapitan Heinrich von Nostitz und Janckendorf, credit for taking prisoners during wartime and risking his own mission by doing so. More often than not, the U-boat commanders demonstrated unusually humane tendencies, especially when dealing with crews of sailing vessels. They were also noted for speaking very good English. The following is an excerpt from a statement appearing in a 1920 Navy Department publication entitled *German Submarine Activities on the Atlantic Coast of the United States and Canada* (the chapter is "The Cruise of the U-151"). The excerpt is regarding the four-masted schooner *Hauppauge*, which left Portland, Maine, on May 17 en route to Norfolk, Virginia, for a load of coal. One of the "prisoners" removed from *Hauppauge* on May 25, the mate M.H. Saunders, makes the following observation:

*The food was good. In the morning we had rolls and fresh butter. The butter was fine. The bread was black and came in loaves about 3 feet long. We had cognac nearly all the time.*

*They had three gramophones on board. The members of the crew were cheerful and joked with us, especially after indulging in cognac. They were apparently young fellows and frequently talked of their mothers.*

June 2, 1918, is known as "Black Sunday" to many connoisseurs of maritime history. This is the day Captain Heinrich and his *U-151* sank six U.S. ships within twelve hours. The first to go was the Bath-built three-masted schooner *Isabel B. Wiley* as she headed for Newport News, Virginia, to load coal. In waters off the coast of New Jersey, at 7:50 a.m., the captain came on deck and noticed a "suspicious looking object about 1,200 yards away." The craft was, of course, *U-151*, and the captain and his crew were ordered to evacuate the schooner. Here is some detail from the statement of the *Wiley*'s master, Captain Thom Thomassen:

*When about 1,000 yards off the submarine fired a shot that fell about 100 yards of the vessel. I then went below and got an American ensign, came on deck, and hoisted it. Then I hove my vessel to and hauled down the jibs.*

After his ship was boarded, Captain Thomassen was instructed to leave the vessel with his crew in the lifeboat and also to take on some of the prisoners who had been detained in the submarine. Captain Thomassen recalls the following:

*Before shoving off from the submarine I informed the captain that I did not have sufficient water to take care of the extra men, and he gave me a large keg of water.*

*I did not see the* Wiley *blown up, but about one hour afterwards I heard three distinct explosions.*

The next ship to be blown up was the steam freighter *Winneconne* at about 9:15 a.m. Sufficient time was given to the crew to allow them to evacuate the vessel aboard lifeboats. Near Barnegat Light off the New Jersey coast, the four-masted schooner *Jacob M. Haskell* was making her way toward Boston with a hold full of coal when shots were fired across her bow. Again, the crew members of the schooner were allowed to leave their vessel in the lifeboat. Captain William H. Davis, master of the *Haskell*, reported:

*Upon leaving the ship we were allowed to take our valuables, the chronometer, the sextant, and some sailing charts.*

*A few minutes later the Haskell was blown up and disappeared with all sails set. As we were starting on our way, the boarding officer called out:*

*"Good luck. The New Jersey coast is just 40 miles away. Better go there."*

Interestingly, there was another schooner captain from Maine named Davis, and he was also at sea at this time in the four-masted schooner *Maude Palmer*. Captain Stinson Davis, brother to Captain William Davis, divulged the following during an interview for *Down East* magazine that appeared in the August 1978 issue:

*The German U-boats were thick. Why, a submarine sunk my brother's ship right off Barnegat Bay, New Jersey, and two days later, I sailed right through the wreckage, coming up from South America with a load of timber. My brother, William H. Davis, was eight years older than me. We grew up together and we both went to sea. On this voyage he had the* Jacob M. Haskell, *and was bound for New York from Norfolk, Virginia with coal. They was eatin' dinner and the cook went down and says, "Captain, there's a German submarine along side of us!" My brother went out on deck and the captain of the sub calls to him, "We'll give ya five minutes to get out." Captain Davis says back to him, "Pretty short order, isn't it? Five minutes?" So the German say he'll give him seven minutes. By the time my brother and his crew were in the yawl boat, the Germans had put a time bomb on the* Haskell. *They didn't want to waste a torpedo on her.*

The *Jacob M. Haskell* was built in Rockland, Maine, and launched in 1901. She was sister ship to the *Edward H. Cole*, built in Rockland in 1904. Both schooners were owned by Crowell & Thurlow of Boston. Coincidentally, the *Edward H. Cole* was to be the next victim of *U-151*. According to the U.S. Navy publication, H.G. Newcomb was master of the schooner *Cole*, and he reported the following:

*We sailed from Norfolk, Va., on May 30, for Portland, Me., with a cargo of 2,516 tons of coal. I might not have been on the regular steamship course, as I had to follow God's good winds. At 3:10 in the afternoon of June 2, when about 50 miles southeast of Barnegat Light, we sighted a boat on the starboard bow about 2,000 yards away. She circled around and came aft on the port quarter. When she came pretty close I put the glasses on her and saw it was a German flag she was flying. She came up then about 150 feet off us and told us to clear away the boats, as they were going to sink us, which we did.*

The fifth vessel to fall prey to *U-151* was the steam freighter *Texel*. Stopped after three warning shots were fired over her, the *Texel*'s crew members were allowed to get away in lifeboats before their vessel was sunk. The final sinking of the day was the passenger liner *Carolina*, headed to New York with 218 passengers and a crew of 117. The *Carolina* had something the schooners didn't have: a wireless. Just as the wireless operator was going to send an SOS giving their position, the submarine wired them a message: "If you don't use the wireless, I won't shoot." The crew and passengers of the *Carolina* were allowed to use their lifeboats and were eventually rescued by the coastal schooner *Eva B. Douglas*. Captain Barber of the *Carolina* recounts the following:

*At 11 a.m. June 3, I sighted a schooner standing to the northward and sent the second officer's boat to intercept her. We saw her haul down her jibs and heave to. I ordered all the boats to proceed to the schooner, which proved to be the* Eva B. Douglas. *Capt. G. Launo, master of the schooner, and his wife and daughter received us with fine courtesy and placed all their supplies and stores at our disposal.*

"Black Sunday" drew to a close with six ships sunk by *U-151*, including three Maine coastal schooners, and produced only thirteen casualties. The unfortunate deaths were the result of one the *Carolina*'s lifeboats capsizing in an evening squall. The United States was at war with Germany, and Captain Heinrich had only just begun. On Monday, June 3, he sent another Maine schooner to the bottom of the Atlantic, the four-masted *Samuel C. Mengel*.

Many, many schooners were sunk during this time in history, but the *Mengel* is deserving of note. She was built by Percy & Small in Bath and was launched on January 13, 1917. She was the only craft built at that yard that was equipped with an auxiliary power source, twin steam engines. What is of the most interest, however, is that the engines were removed less than a year after the *Mengel* went into service, and she was turned into a true windjammer. The reason for this "modification" was due to the fact that the engines weren't operating consistently, the engine equipment was taking up one-sixth of the hull and the propellers were a considerable drag on the ship when she was under sail.

Captain H.T. Hansen was master of the *Samuel C. Mengel* on Monday, June 3, 1918. At about six o'clock that evening, a shot was fired across the bow of the schooner, and *U-151* came alongside, a German officer instructing the crew to abandon ship. The officer instructed Captain Hansen to take plenty of bread and water with them on the yawl boat and to make sure that they brought heavy clothing in case the weather turned bad. According to a *New York Times* article published on June 6, 1918:

> *Captain Hansen said that the U-boat commander asked for the ship's papers and kept them, and when he remonstrated at being set adrift in an open boat 125 miles from land the German replied:*
>
> *"That's all right, Captain. Have no fear. The water is warm, the weather fine, and there are plenty of ships passing to pick you up. Good luck."*

In *U-151*'s ninety-four-day cruise along the northeast coast, Captain Heinrich sank twenty-three ships and laid mines that resulted in the sinking of several additional vessels. The world was at war. There were several U-boats searching for prey along the U.S. coast, and many American vessels were sunk. There are many incidents worthy of note; one in particular, which was reported in the *New York Times* on July 24, 1918, is especially interesting. The article was entitled "U-Boat Sinks Ship off Maine Coast" and reported that a fishing schooner, the *Robert & Richard*, was sunk, the U-boat sending a warning shot over the bow first. The master of the schooner, Captain Wharton, disclosed the following unbelievable information about the incident:

> *As soon as the Germans came up within hailing distance three men—the commander, first officer, and a seaman—came on deck. The first officer ordered us to send a boat alongside. I went over in my boat and rowed the three Germans to the schooner and boarded her with them. Both officers spoke good English but had little to say. The first officer, however, loosened up a bit. He went down into the cabin to get the ship's papers and the American flag I kept there.*
>
> *When he came up on deck he said: "This is the second American flag I have now. I have one in my summer home in Maine, and I'll keep this to go with it some day." I opened my eyes at this statement and asked him if he*

*lived in Maine. He had lived in America a long time, he told me, and had a summer home in Maine since 1896.*

There were many defensive strategies employed by the United States to thwart the efforts of the German U-boat commanders. Mines and depth charges were used, aircraft patrols were tried, underwater listening devices were invented and searchlights and, unbelievably, "anti-submarine nets" were among some of the tactics and devices used. A simple convoy of a group of ships, however, was most effective. There were also armed trawlers and "Q" boats, the latter a vessel masquerading as a merchant ship but carrying concealed guns. Sailing vessels were often utilized for this purpose, as we can see from this excerpt from *Our Navy in the War*, published in 1919 by Lawrence Perry:

*The schooner, commanded by a Maine skipper and his crew, was turned loose in the North Sea. Astern towed a dingy; from the taffrail flew the American flag. Before long out popped a submarine. Aha! A lumber-laden vessel—American! The German commander, grinning broadly, stepped into a gig with a bombing crew; torpedoes were not wasted on sailing vessels.*

*"Get into your dingy," he cried, motioning toward the craft dangling astern.*

*The Maine skipper, in his red underclothes, besought, and then cursed—while the German grinned the more broadly. Finally, however, the irate skipper and his crew of five clambered into their dingy as ordered by the commander of the submarine. And then! No sooner had the schooner crew cleared the windjammer than the deck-load of lumber resolved itself into a series of doors, and out of each door protruded a gun. It was the last of that submarine, of course.*

# Luther Little and Hesper

The strange connection between Maine schooners and Somerset, Massachusetts, doesn't end with the *Governor Ames* and the Davis family. Instead, it ends deep in the muck next to what remains of an old dock along the Sheepscot River in Wiscasset, Maine. The most famous Maine schooners of all, the Wiscasset Schooners (the *Luther Little* and *Hesper*), weren't built in Maine. Most of the millions and millions of people who passed by them on U.S. Route 1, both tourists and Mainers alike, assumed that the ships had originated in Maine. It was the natural thing to do. As a child growing up in Maine, I also thought the schooners that had occupied the same spot along the edge of the Sheepscot River in Wiscasset were built in Maine.

Maybe they weren't made in Maine, but they had certainly become Maine. The Maine wind, tides and weather tempered the schooners as they sat aground in the Sheepscot for sixty-six years. The schooners had become as much Maine as the Sheepscot River itself or anything else could be.

It is often necessary to become acquainted with the beginning as well as the end of a thing in order to understand it fully, to comprehend the impact it had on those whose lives it influenced and to see the larger picture. In order to accomplish this, one must be able to envision the history as a whole.

Located on the Taunton River, Somerset has been home to shipbuilding since 1694, and the first commercial shipyard was built in 1695. Since then, hundreds of vessels have been built on Somerset shores. The shipbuilding boom that occurred during World War I was no exception, and by 1916 a Somerset shipbuilder had a contract to build a four-masted schooner. She was to be named *Luther Little*, after one of the members of the Boston firm

# From Glory Days to Ghost Ships

Looking aft from the galley
aboard the *Luther Little*. *Courtesy of
Lawrence Lufkin.*

that ordered the construction. The following year, another four-masted
schooner was to be built, and she would be named *Hesper*, the evening star
in Greek mythology. Interestingly, Hesper (or the variation Hesperus), being
the evening star as opposed to the morning star, also has the connotation of
representing the end of something. It was even considered by some to be the
star of death, and *Hesperus* was the name of the schooner that met her end
so terribly in Longfellow's famous poem of the same name.

According to everything that I had ever read on the subject, the *Luther Little*
was built by Read Brothers Shipbuilding of Somerset and was launched in
December 1917. The *Hesper* was built about a year later at Crowinshield
Shipbuilding Company in south Somerset, Massachusetts. I had been
studying these ships for years, and I thought I knew the facts. Actually, it
seemed quite clear: two ships and two shipyards, one launched in 1917 and
the other in 1918. Was there any more to the story? I knew that if I was
going to seriously research these vessels I needed more help from the folks at
the Somerset Historical Society.

"The *Luther Little* was built by Read Brothers," I declared. "And she was
launched December 20, 1917."

Below deck aboard the *Luther Little*, looking toward stern, circa 1975. *Courtesy of Lawrence Lufkin.*

"Well, we're not quite sure about that," Somerset Historical Society president Diane Goodwin responded, smiling. "There was a fire at Read Brothers, and it destroyed a four-masted schooner that had been named *Luther Little*."

"A fire destroyed the *Luther Little*? When? Were two ships named *Luther Little*?" I asked, completely confused and not so certain about anything anymore.

"The *Luther Little* that you are talking about, the one that was in Maine, was really the second *Luther Little*. If we want facts, we will have to visit the Fall River Public Library and spend some time in the research room looking through the newspaper archives," Diane informed me. "Are you up to it?"

"Yes," I replied, my heartbeat already becoming more rapid. There was a mystery to be solved, the game was afoot and I was ready. "I'd love to go."

The Fall River Public Library is an impressive four-story stone structure with an extensive stairway leading up to heavy glass doors that are reinforced with brass. Etched on a massive stone slab above the main entrance were the words "The People's University." The research room occupies the fourth floor, and it is at the end of what seems to be an endless, winding stairway. I presumed that Fall River liked to keep its historians well exercised. The nice man at the desk told us that we could help ourselves to the canisters of microfilm that contained the *Fall River Evening News* archives from the last century.

"When was the *Luther Little* launched?" Diane asked.

"December of 1917," I replied.

"Do you know what day?"

"December 1? No, that was the *Governor Ames*. Sorry," I apologized. I knew that meant we would have to look through every issue of the *Evening News* until we found what we were looking for.

"It's okay, we'll just look at the whole month," she said, skillfully feeding the microfilm into the maze of rollers and slots that composed the only accessible portion of the viewing machine.

It was interesting to see the news of December 1917. It was clear there was a war going on, and news about the "Great War" or the "War to End All Wars" flowed freely through the pages. There were reports of German submarines sinking steamers and other vessels on nearly every front page. The Atlantic Ocean during this time was quite an exciting place, as U-boats were turning up everywhere, stalking merchant vessels in an attempt to cut the supply lines between North America and Britain, sinking every ship they could. Finally, on the first page of the Thursday, December 20, 1917 edition of the *Fall River Evening News*:

*LAUNCHING AT LAST A REALITY*
*Four-Masted Luther Little Plunges into the water at 12:32 P.M.*

*After being twice postponed, the launching of the four-masted schooner, Luther Little, became an accomplished fact at 12:32 today. The great ship took to the water gracefully, plunging 17 feet into the deep when first leaving the ways, then coming to the surface, rocking gently, and finally settling in her home element, riding as gracefully as a swan.*

*Miss Barbara Hoyt of New York, daughter of James K Hoyt of New York, business partner of Luther Little, after whom the ship is named, christened the ship, breaking the gaily bedecked bottle of champagne over her bows a few seconds before the graceful hulk slid into the river. "I christen thee Luther Little," said Miss Hoyt, as the bottle was dashed in pieces. An instant later the last chock was split from under the ship, and she settled into the water.*

*There were people present who have seen many launchings, and all agreed that never had one been accomplished in a smoother manner. The water was as calm as that in a mill pond, and scarcely a ripple stirred as the ship was released from the ways and settled in the water.*

*The launching was the culmination of many months of work, and the Crowninshield Shipbuilding Company has overcome many obstacles in building this big schooner. The predecessors of the Crowninshields in Somerset, the Read Brothers, built the first Luther Little, which was destroyed last February before being completed. Immediately after the burning the second craft was begun, and work on her has been rushed since that time. A force of over 100 men has been working, under the able direction of Leader Blinn as foreman, ever since the keel was laid, and the workmen were present this morning and raised a loud cheer as the big ship slid gracefully into the water. The men who worked faithfully and well to build this valuable acquisition to Uncle Sam's carrying forces have the satisfaction of knowing that they have contributed materially to the defeat of the Kaiser, for the slogan "Food will win the war," is coming more and more to be recognized as a keynote of the situation.*

By 1917, the story of the wind ships would have just about passed into recent history, and if it wasn't for the shipping demands brought about by the war, there they would likely have remained. Unearthed by the unique circumstances created by the war, including an increased need for inexpensively built and manned merchant vessels, the war also provided an unlikely reprieve for the age of sail. One can detect a sort of pride, a feeling of goodwill that the public had toward these vessels. Below is another excerpt from the same article:

*Captain William P. Richardson, the veteran skipper, who is to command the Little, was on hand supervising the arrangements, and his first mate, J.R. McDonald, another veteran of storm and gale, was also a very busy man, attending to a multitude of details in the imperturbable manner of the men who go to sea in ships. These officers, together with the crew, were polite and even stretched a point to be courteous, but at times they had a hard time to conceal their amusement at the vastness of the ignorance of the landlubbers who bumped about here and there on the good ship, speaking of the deck as the "floor," of going into the "kitchen," when they meant galley, and of going downstairs when they meant they were going "below," of walls when they meant bulkheads, and so on, to the great disgust of the seafaring men.*

*High water was at 12:33, and the nicety with which everything was done can be seen when it is stated that it was just 12:32 that the schooner took to the water. As she slid into the briny deep her own whistle screeched in triumph and was answered by the whistles of all other ships nearby, the tug Cohannet doing the yeoman work with her siren. Just as the Little glided into the water the Cohannet put away from the wharf nearby, and warped her alongside the wharf.*

*The Little is to be fully provisioned, and is nearly ready for her maiden voyage, which will be to Hampton Roads. She will carry coal to Buenos*

*Aires, and on her return trip will bring a cargo of linseed, which will be pressed and have the oil extracted in this country. Linseed oil is very scarce now, and is in great demand.*

*Now that the Luther Little has been launched, all energies of the Crowinshield Shipping Company will be bent on completing the Hesper, the sister ship of the Little, which, however, is a trifle larger than the ship just launched.*

A few pages later, in the same Thursday, December 20, 1917 edition, was an article entitled "Farewell Reception," and it was regarding Mrs. William P. Richardson of Camden, Maine, wife of the captain of the *Luther Little*. It would seem that the ship launching in Somerset would also influence folks next door in Fall River, as Mrs. Albert T. Borden entertained members of her Sunday school class from the Baptist Temple in conjunction with hosting a farewell reception for the captain's wife. Mrs. Richardson had apparently been connected with the Sunday school in some way and was given a floral plaque by Mrs. Borden. After supper, the group enjoyed ice cream and cake, after which Miss Ada Chace played the piano and Miss Helen Borden the violin. It would seem that Mrs. Richardson would be going to sea with her husband very soon.

The research up to this point had certainly been successful, and a lot of information that likely hadn't seen the light of day for over ninety years had just been liberated from its dusty archival sepulcher. It was both rewarding and exciting to have found this wealth of information, and I knew that I had the president of the historical society to thank. What other treasures could we find hidden within that drawer of microfilm?

"What about the fire?" I asked.

"Let's look it up while we're here. This article says the fire was last February."

"February of 1917," I replied.

"Right. I'll get the microfilm; we'll have to check through the whole month again as it doesn't give a date."

The article was easily located, as it was on the front page. Although the fire took place late on Saturday, February 17, 1917, it wasn't reported in the *Fall River Evening News* until Monday, February 19, 1917. The *Evening News* was not published on Sundays. The headline jumped right out at us:

*FIRE WIPES OUT READ SHIPYARD*
*Four Master Luther Little, on the stocks, is totally destroyed.*

*Read Brothers' shipyard at South Somerset was reduced to ashes by a fire which broke out in the boiler room late Saturday afternoon. The entire plant was razed by flames and the four-masted schooner, Luther Little, which was in the process of construction at the yard, was totally destroyed.*

*The fire rapidly ate its way from building to building, until the whole yard was given up to flames. From the boilerhouse the fire went through the mill, boatshop, which was one of the largest buildings in the yard, the caulking loft, the blacksmith shop, paint shop, stock room, another big building, office, and watchman's house. In a remarkably short time the yard was a raging furnace, and fanned by the southeast wind the fire rapidly neared the big schooner.*

*Once getting a grip on the unfinished craft, the flames soon ran her entire length. Within a few minutes from the time she caught, the vessel was doomed. From stem to stern, the fire enveloped her, roaring and snapping like a devil's inferno. It was a thrilling sight to watch the awful destruction wrought on the network of timbers and planking, but it seemed pitiful that a proud vessel should come to such an end.*

So there definitely were two schooners named *Luther Little*, not just one, and there was just one shipyard, not two. Crowninshield Shipbuilding Company took over the Read Shipyard after the February fire, and neither of the Wiscasset Schooners was built by Read Brothers.

Interestingly, the headline just after the Read Shipyard article was entitled "French Liner Sinks U-Boat." It seems they had hidden weapons aboard the ship. On the following page, there was an interesting bit entitled "Urges Turning Clock Back." This article stated that Marcus M. Marks, president of the National Daylight Saving Association, announced that he had written to President Wilson urging him to expedite for passage the Gallinger-Borland Bill, which provided for turning the clock forward one hour during summer months. On the same page, there was also an obituary for a Civil War hero who was severely wounded in the Battle of Chancellorsville and who had been awarded a Congressional Medal for gallantry. That was just some of the news for Monday, February 19, 1917.

I knew that the *Hesper* was supposed to have been launched on the Fourth of July in 1918, but something happened and she got stuck on the ways. When was she really launched? It was time to get the microfiche canister for July 1918. As World War I didn't end until the armistice on the eleventh hour of the eleventh day of the eleventh month, in July 1918 the United

The *Luther Little* on the stocks in 1917 at Crowinshield Shipbuilding Company in Somerset, Massachusetts. Her builders pose proudly in the foreground. *Courtesy of Boothbay Region Historical Society.*

States was still very much at war. Although understandably engrossed in the business of the world's current hostilities, the folks who read the *Fall River Evening News* were very much like we are today. An ad for hair dye caught my eye: "No More Gray Hair" it promised. "Excelsior Hair Dye is instantaneous and restores hair to its natural shade." It was also "guaranteed harmless" and promised not to wash out. Just below that was an endorsement for "Old Mill Coffee," which cost "30 cents the pound." As if that wasn't enough, the ad further stated that you could "bring 15 empty bags to your grocer and get one full bag free." Right next to that on the same page in the Friday, July 5, 1918 edition were the following words:

SCHOONER HESPER STICKS ON WAYS
*Keen Disappointment For Spectators of Expected Launching*

*The thousands of people who lined both shores of the Taunton River Thursday afternoon, to watch the launching of the four-masted schooner Hesper of 2200 tons from the Crowinshield yards in South Somerset suffered keen disappointment, but not half so keen as that of the builders, when the handsome vessel, after a thrilling start, stopped suddenly just as her rudder entered the water.*

*Though a thundershower threatened in the early afternoon, the crowds began to gather several hours before the time announced, and long lines of automobiles gathered in the vicinity, while off the yard was assembled one of the largest fleet of yachts seen in this bay in many years. Vantage points on the Fall River shore as well as on the Somerset side of the river were thronged, and a large number of guests were admitted to the yard. The schooner was open to inspection and was looked over from forecastle to captain's cabin by hundreds of admirers. The ship was gaily decorated with bunting, including the banner of the United States Shipping boards.*

*The wedging-up preparatory to the launching started shortly before 5 o'clock, followed by the knocking away of the blocking, starting at the stern. As the workmen under the keel advanced the shoring on either side was also removed and when they had reached the bow, about 12 minutes before 6, the ship began to move and was christened with a bottle of champagne, tied with the national colors, by Mrs. Herman Livingstone Greendale of New York, wife of one of the largest owners in the ship.*

*The vessel started nobly, amid the blare of the whistle at the works, and the cheers of the throng, but after sliding swiftly, perhaps 40 feet, toward the water, lost speed and stopped, and all hope of getting her into the water that day had to be abandoned.*

*An elaborate luncheon was served in the mould loft to the invited guests. Congressman Greene made an address before the knocking away of the blocking began.*

*The Hesper, which was built for the offshore trade, for Rogers & Webb of Boston, is 195 feet long on the keel, 41 feet beam and 20 feet depth of hold. She was built by Crowninshields for government service and cost $150,000. Captain C.A. Haskell of Maine, formerly master of the schooner George S. Smith, is to command the vessel.*

Looking over the *Evening News* for the rest of the month of July proved fruitless, unless one considers the vast wealth of information that can be gleaned simply by perusing the news of the day. On Thursday, August 22, 1918, there was talk of a body recovered from the harbor near a coal dock in Fall River, another fishing schooner was sunk by a U-boat near Cape Breton, a cart horse tried to enter a house while making deliveries and the schooner *Hesper* launched herself. Yes, *Hesper* did seem to have a mind of her own:

*Well, Schooner Hesper's Launched*
*Floats Free at Flood Tide After Being Stuck Since Fourth of July*

*The recently constructed four-masted schooner Hesper finally floated free of the bottom at Crowninshield's shipyard of her own accord at flood tide at 8:22 o'clock this morning and she is now tied up to the shipyard wharf awaiting the arrival of her owners who have been notified of the good news.*

*The vessel was in readiness for launching on July 4, and a record-breaking crowd gathered to witness the spectacle, but for some unknown reason after starting down the ways the craft brought up short. Almost daily efforts have been made since to get the schooner off her ways, both tugs and hydraulic jacks being used at different times, and though she was pulled entirely off her ways, it was not until this morning that she floated free.*

*The schooner is the second four-master to be launched from the yard since the beginning of the war.*

The careers of these two four-masted schooners weren't exactly glamorous, nor were they much different from that of their brethren. They transported coal, hauled manure and survived any way they could. Their wooden hulls were punished mercilessly by the sea and often overloaded with heavy cargo. They were intended to be commercial haulers of freight and nothing more.

The *Luther Little* was just over 204 feet long and just under 41 feet wide. Although not as large as many of the big coasters, she was still a big ship. The *Luther* encountered a bit of excitement early in her career while under the command of her first master, Captain William P. Richardson. In June 1918, near the coast of Delaware, her crew rescued two balloonists from New Jersey whom they saw crash into the sea! Both men and the balloon were taken aboard and brought safely to the next port. In July 1920, the *Luther* ran aground at Fort Liberte Harbor, Haiti, deeply loaded with logwood that was bound for Pennsylvania, and was stuck there for more than two weeks.

The launching of the *Luther Little* at Crowninshield Shipyard on December 20, 1917. *Courtesy of Somerset Historical Society.*

A *Luther Little* deck view showing masts and rigging, with schooner *Hesper* lying beside. *Courtesy of Lawrence Lufkin.*

Luckily, she was pulled off without extensive damage, or there she would have remained for eternity. As cargoes became more and more difficult to find, the *Luther* was tied up to a dock or lay at anchor more than she worked. Eventually, the *Luther Little* ended up lying idle in Portland Harbor, doing nothing but swinging on her anchor chain.

*Hesper* was just over 210 feet long and 41 feet wide. She crossed the Atlantic often, bringing coal to Lisbon and case oil to France, often returning to the states with fertilizer from Venezuela. In February 1920, *Hesper* left Norfolk, Virginia, with two thousand tons of coal for Boston. She made Martha's Vineyard on March 4 but never made it to Boston. Instead, she encountered a nasty spring gale that tore her sails and drove her off course. She limped into Portland Harbor five days later, where she remained until her sails could be replaced. In February 1925, she had a bit of bad luck in Boston Harbor, where she caught her anchor in some muck and had to be cut free of it. Her anchor may still lie at the bottom of Boston Harbor. One month later and heavily loaded with lumber, she got her bottom stuck in Boston Harbor! It took nine tugboats to pull her free, and she was, not surprisingly, strained from the incident.

Below deck aboard the *Hesper*, circa 1975. *Courtesy of Lawrence Lufkin.*

In January 1928, *Hesper*, always a bit feisty, demolished a pier during a nor'easter while she was tied up in Rockport, Maine. She tore her wharf apart, leaving timbers and planks in her wake, and was blown onto the beach with amazingly little damage done to herself. The Rockport pier owners were anxious to get rid of her, and the *Hesper* was towed to Portland Harbor, where she remained until 1932.

Neither ship would ever again return to Massachusetts. Instead, the two schooners, sister ships, *Luther Little* and *Hesper*, would be forever associated with the state of Maine, becoming famous landmarks in the town of Wiscasset.

# The Magic of the
# Wiscasset Schooners

An enterprising fellow named Frank Winter from Auburn, Maine, owned considerable timber lots "up north" in Palermo, Maine. Although the country was in the throes of the Great Depression, Mr. Winter had an idea for an entrepreneurial venture that would change the face of the Wiscasset waterfront and leave an indelible mark on Maine history—just not in the way he imagined. In 1930, he purchased the defunct Wiscasset, Waterville & Farmington narrow-gauge railway to transport his timber, but he also needed schooners to bring his cargoes into the ports of Boston and New York.

In 1932, after making much-needed repairs to the railway and rebuilding part of the wharf in Wiscasset, Frank Winter visited Portland Harbor with the intention of acquiring his ships. At this time, it was becoming very difficult to find cargoes for sailing vessels, and the vessels could be purchased cheaply. In June, Mr. Winter purchased two handsome schooners that had been at anchor for a few years near Portland's Eastern Promenade. The maintenance bills were adding up, and they were being auctioned off to settle claims against them. He paid $525 for the smaller vessel and $600 for the larger and had them towed to Wiscasset. They were, of course, the *Luther Little* and the *Hesper*.

The schooners were maintained, painted and repaired, and *Luther* became home to a captain and his family for a short period. *Hesper* was home to a young man who had been hired by Frank Winter to paint and do some repair work on her. The vessels were being readied for use. Interestingly, Mr. Winter originally intended to use the ships as barges, towing them into ports.

The Wiscasset Schooners in winter. *Courtesy of Lawrence Lufkin.*

The ships must have worked their magic on him, though, being in proximity to them. He decided to sail the schooners instead.

Before his plans could come to fruition, however, the railway he had purchased only a few years earlier began to encounter problems. There were mechanical failures as well as accidents, including the death of a Wiscasset man who fell from the railway trestle and drowned in a tidal pool. The numerous catastrophes became insurmountable, and it became clear that the schooners would never sail again. A watchman lived aboard the vessels until 1936, after which time they were dragged closer to shore and abandoned. The *Hesper* had begun to list considerably toward her port side, which faced the *Luther*. This caused her masts to come quite close to shore, possibly creating a safety hazard. A shipbreaker came from Portland and removed *Hesper*'s masts, windlass and steam hoisting engine in 1940, leaving her nothing more than a barren hulk.

In 1945, the ships were set afire during the festivities in conjunction with the ending of World War II, but the blaze was extinguished. Nonetheless, fire remained a threat throughout the existence of the vessels, and from time to time the Wiscasset Fire Department valiantly doused the hazard. In 1970, *Hesper*'s fore cabin became the victim of a carelessly tossed cigarette.

As time marched on and the age of the sailing ship became further and further removed from daily life, the aging schooners became a tourist

A *Luther Little* photo taken from the *Hesper* deck, showing evidence of her ghostly journey through time. *Courtesy of Lawrence Lufkin.*

attraction. The stage was set: two weather-beaten wooden-hulled sailing vessels lying aground beside rotted docks against the backdrop of the Sheepscot River in Wiscasset, Maine. The audience: all who passed along coastal U.S. Route 1 from 1932 until 1998. Nearly everybody who drove through Wiscasset succumbed to their strange magic.

They were really no longer the *Luther Little* and the *Hesper*. Instead, they were the Wiscasset Schooners, lying in shallow water along the edge of the Sheepscot River near the old railway. They weren't famous because of the number of masts they carried, the length of hull or beam, the configuration of their sails, cargo capacity or due to something innovative in their construction. They became famous due to the high visibility of their final berth; they became celebrated because they were ghosts you could see. They were ghosts you could walk right up to and photograph. A mecca of travel for the hordes of tourists who descend on Maine en masse during the clement months, U.S. Coastal Route 1 provided a fast-paced mechanized society with a gateway into the past, a porthole back to the much romanticized age of sail.

The Wiscasset Schooners as they appeared during the mid-'70s. *Courtesy of Lawrence Lufkin.*

It is no surprise that the schooners became the most photographed ships in Maine, New England and in all of North America. There were also vast quantities of postcards created that depicted the schooners in all sorts of weather conditions, as well as different times of day, including moonlight shots. These postcards all touted the state of Maine, portraying vessels that lingered near a dock in Wiscasset. The Somerset schooners had become Wiscasset, Maine schooners, and they enchanted practically everybody who saw them.

To explain the magic of these vessels, one does not need to do exhaustive research, consult any psychology journals or conduct time-consuming interviews. I know firsthand. I was there. It goes beyond "history"; it gets deep inside you and you can't shake it. It just lingers there and then lies dormant until it is reawakened over and over.

It was a sweltering summer afternoon, as hot as it can get in Maine, and I was just four years old. My parents, grandparents and I were heading home on U.S. Route 1 after being at a clambake all day. I was quite unhappy as I disliked seafood, especially clams and lobster, and wasn't having a good day at all. On the ride back, I had refused to talk and was staring out of the rear window of my parents' Ford. That's when I first saw them.

"Ships! Look at the old ships!" I exclaimed suddenly. "Look! Look!" I screamed, gazing longingly at the *Luther Little* with her tall masts and rigging still attached, imagining that ghost sailors might emerge from the fo'c'sle at any moment.

"Quiet down," my mother scolded, ineffectively, while my father cast a deprecating stare in my direction.

"Look! Look!" I continued to yell, and then, "Stop! Stop! I have to see the ships!"

"Let her see the old schooners," my grandfather replied. "What harm can it do?"

Rather than allow a four-year-old to bounce and scream uncontrollably in the back seat, my parents likely assumed it would be better to indulge me.

I couldn't take my eyes off them; it was as if I recognized them. There was the smell of low tide, a hot summer breeze, seagulls and the schooners silhouetted against the backdrop of Sheepscot Bay in Wiscasset. Finally, my parents pulled me away and tossed me into the backseat of the Galaxie 500, my head hanging out of the window, longingly staring back as the car sped away. I watched the schooners disappear but never forgot them. It

The bow of the *Luther Little* showing her age. *Courtesy of Lawrence Lufkin.*

wasn't merely curiosity about the past that made me stare at the schooners, spellbound and beguiled. It was something else, something even stronger. I had just seen a ghost. There was something in the old ships—something that was in me, too. It was intrinsic to life itself. Perhaps it is the struggle to tenaciously cling to the fight when the battle seems already lost that resonates so poignantly in our heart and touches our soul, or maybe it's merely morbid curiosity about what we, too, will one day become.

Since the schooners were so frequently photographed, there is certainly no shortage of images of them. Not surprisingly, however, the majority of the photographs are those that have been taken from shore. With the exception of a few aerial views and some photos taken from boats on the Sheepscot River, there really aren't many other images available. Fortunately, we do have the photographs of Lawrence Lufkin. In the early 1970s, when the ships were still with us, a young photographer from nearby Winslow, Maine, decided to photograph them. This was very fortunate, indeed, because Mr. Lufkin wasn't the sort of photographer who could be satisfied with simply taking the same shots that millions of other folks had taken over the years. While the ships were still there, he wanted to record their presence more thoroughly and capture them more intimately.

The only cargo the *Luther* carries below her rotted decks is the sea. *Courtesy of Lawrence Lufkin.*

I had the pleasure of meeting Mr. Lufkin at his home in Tiverton, Rhode Island, not very far from Somerset, Massachusetts, where the schooners were built. A longtime maritime enthusiast, Mr. Lufkin's home was filled with pictures of clipper ships, the *Titanic* and many of his photographs of the Wiscasset Schooners.

"I just stood there on the shore looking up at the ships," Mr. Lufkin explained, shaking his head. "This isn't doing it, I thought. This is not doing it. I wanted to go aboard the vessels. I wanted to get the views you couldn't get from the shore."

"You certainly accomplished that," I said. "You succeeded in photographing a ghost while it was still among us."

"It wasn't easy," he explained.

A view from the bowsprit on *Luther Little*, looking aft. *Courtesy of Lawrence Lufkin.*

# From Glory Days to Ghost Ships

*I had to use a rubber raft to get out there. And then I had to figure out when it was high tide and when I would be able to paddle out to the schooners, and then how long I could stay aboard. I tied the rubber dinghy up to the* Hesper, *in between the ships, and then I climbed up the side of the* Luther Little. *The rail was gone at that spot so I climbed up the scupper. The deck was so rotted you had to be really careful where you stepped.*

As I listened to this wonderful man explain how much trouble he went through to get some of the shots on the deck of the *Luther Little*, I realized how lucky we were to have his photographic record. He was likely one of the last people to board the schooners and walk on their decks, however rotted they might have been in place.

*Hesper* deck looking toward stern, dismasted and forlorn in the '70s. *Courtesy of Lawrence Lufkin.*

"In order to get some of the best shots, I had to climb up onto the bowsprit and sort of shimmy my way backward, balancing there. I had to be careful," he explained. "And oh," he said, raising his hands and smiling. "And I was almost arrested by the Wiscasset Police! I didn't know it was against the law to go aboard the schooners. They were yelling at me from shore using a bullhorn. 'You on the boat,' they called. 'Report to shore at once!'"

One of the photographs taken aboard the *Luther Little*, from Lufkin's vantage point perched on the bowsprit, earned him a visit to the White House. In the early '70s, during the Nixon administration, the photograph was sent as a gift to First Lady Pat Nixon. Subsequently, Mr. Lufkin was invited to the White House.

During World War I, when expectant guests were walking across the decks of the newly built ships at their launching in Somerset, the schooners created a sensation. At the time photographer Lawrence Lufkin climbed aboard, careful not to step through the rotted planking on the deck, the schooners had created a sentiment of another sort.

The Wiscasset Schooners are gone now. The tired vessels lingered as long as they could, eventually leaning against each other, together in death as they were at their birth. Perhaps unable to bear the thought of existing in the twenty-first century, the schooners finally weakened and collapsed into the sea. In 1998, when the remains of the hulks were cleared away from the waterfront, all that remained was a pile of indistinguishable rubble. A portion of what remains of the *Luther Little* and *Hesper*, some iron pieces and other small items used on the vessels, now lie in a glass case at the Somerset Historical Society.

# Schooner Bones

## Boothbay and the Ghost Fleet

Traveling north on U.S. Coastal Route 1 en route to the Boothbay Region Historical Society, I passed through Bath, Maine. The sign was an impressive one, I thought, as I entered city limits. It depicted a six-masted schooner under full sail, and the caption read, "Entering Bath, Maine. The City of Ships." Just afterward, I saw a sign that directed interested travelers to the Maine Maritime Museum, which is located on the site of the Percy & Small Shipyard. When I passed a sign that informed the traveler that they were "Entering Wiscasset," I almost felt as if I was going home. For just a moment, perhaps, I wanted to forget that the schooners were no longer there and turned to look for them as I had done so often in the past. Boothbay isn't very far from Wiscasset, and I was on my way to the historical society hoping to find out more about the schooners that were built there and those that were laid up. I was especially intrigued by the ships that returned to Boothbay to reside in the Mill Cove, the well-known site of the "Dead Fleet," or "Ghost Fleet."

Even ghosts were alive at some point, and the schooners that resided in the ship graveyard at Boothbay—those vessels that came to be known as the Ghost Fleet—were very much vital and thriving during the time that spanned the Great War and shortly afterward. Freight rates soared during the war, making it profitable again to employ wooden-hulled sailing vessels in the commercial trade. Even after the war came to an end in 1918, the need for bringing coal into New England ports did not wane. During the mid-1920s, there was a need to carry lumber south to fuel the Miami building boom. This work kept the schooners going for a while, but there were only so

Some of the Ghost Fleet rafted together in the Mill Cove at Boothbay Harbor. *Courtesy of Boothbay Region Historical Society.*

many shippers willing to give cargoes to sailing vessels and a limited number of men who were willing to man the out-of-date craft.

In Boothbay, shipbuilding was not a new phenomenon and had been well established as an industry since the early 1800s. Well-known builders of fishing boats, topsail schooners, barks, brigs, yachts, sloops, knockabouts, auxiliary schooners, steamships and tugs, Boothbay artisans were no strangers to this vocation. Some three-masted coastal schooners were built in the latter part of the nineteenth century, and there were even two submarine chasers built for the U.S. Navy in 1917. Although Boothbay shipbuilders did turn out two four-masted schooners earlier in their history—the *Elvira J. French* in 1890 and the *Eleanor F. Bartram* in 1903—those built during the shipping boom brought about by World War I are remembered the most. Although the age of commercial sail seemed to be over, the new demand for large merchant ships made Boothbay Harbor shipbuilders comfortable with building large four-masted schooners again. Add to the recipe one more ingredient: the Crowell & Thurlow Steamship Company from Boston. Sort of a misnomer, the Crowell & Thurlow Steamship Company owned eighty-two sailing ships and thirteen steamships in 1923. At the time, it was the

# From Glory Days to Ghost Ships

The *James E. Newsom* at sea. *Author's collection.*

largest owner of wooden sailing vessels in the world, and it was Crowell & Thurlow that put the Boothbay-built schooners to work.

Two major shipyards in Boothbay, the Atlantic Coast Company and the East Coast Company, were formed in 1917 and used exclusively for building and repairing large coastal schooners. The Atlantic Coast Company was formed by Crowell & Thurlow of Boston and turned out six four-masted schooners; the East Coast Company backers included the mayor of Somerville, Massachusetts, and turned out five four-masted schooners.

One of these schooners was the four-master *James E. Newsom*, launched by the East Coast Company on August 23, 1919, and serving in the Crowell & Thurlow fleet. She was named after Boston fruit and produce merchant James E. Newsom and christened by his daughter, Miss Thelma Moss Newsom. The *Newsom* had an interesting and lengthy career; her first cargo consisted of 700,000 feet of lumber to be taken from Boston to Buenos Aires. Spending years ranging up and down the East Coast, early in 1926 the Florida real estate boom found her aground off Miami heavily loaded with 710,000 feet of lumber and lightly damaged. After she went aground again and part of her cargo was removed, a squall came up and battered the craft, driving her ashore. With the seas raging over her decks and part of her hull in splinters, the crew decided to abandon ship. A testament to her robust construction, she was towed away and repaired.

The *Newsom* grounded a few more times, was involved in a collision and lost her rudder in a storm, but she was always able to weather those unfortunate mishaps. The end of her incredibly long career came on May 1, 1942, when she was loaded with salt from Turks Island bound for Nova Scotia and was caught by a German U-boat. She was subsequently shelled and sunk. After the Germans allowed them to escape in the lifeboat, the *Newsom*'s crew found that in their rush to get away they had forgotten to bring the oars, food, water and other necessary items. Unbelievably, the commander of *U-69*, Ulrich Graf, towed the crew back to the schooner to

Schooner *Zebedee E. Cliff* after launching in the fall of 1920. *Author's collection.*

retrieve their supplies, but the cabins of the sinking ship had already begun to fill with seawater. Commander Graf gave the schooner crew a case of rations so they would have ample provisions. *U-69* was lost with all hands in the North Atlantic on February 17, 1943, succumbing to depth charges from British destroyer HMS *Fame*.

On Saturday, November 13, 1920, the 205-foot-long *Zebedee E. Cliff* was the largest and last schooner to be launched from the East Coast Ship Company yard. She was named for the mayor of Somerville, Massachusetts, who was also the president of the company. Mrs. Cliff christened her, though it was during Prohibition, with a bottle of "real" champagne. Sold to Crowell & Thurlow in 1922, the *Cliff* twisted her rudder while bringing six thousand barrels of molasses from New Orleans to Boston. In January 1926, while bound for Miami with a load of lumber, she was rammed by a steamer on her port side opposite the mainmast and nearly became a loss. Her cargo of lumber kept her afloat until she could be towed in for repairs. In 1929, while loading plaster in Nova Scotia, she was caught in an earthquake that twisted her and opened up some of her seams. She was repaired and sent back to find work. By the fall of 1930, she was kept busy bringing Appalachian coal into Maine ports.

The last oceangoing four-master to be launched in the United States was the large *Josiah B. Chase* on January 8, 1921. The *Chase* was built at the Atlantic Coast Company yard in Boothbay. She was 230 feet long, rugged and ready to be put to work, but she lay idle at anchor in the harbor for a bit of time because there weren't any cargoes for her right away.

Although Boothbay Harbor turned out some fine schooners, it is the vessels of the ship graveyard that I will address more attentively. The occupants

Still waiting, the Ghost Fleet is a little the worse for wear. *Left to right*: the *Courtney C. Houck*, the *Zebedee E. Cliff* and the *Freeman* behind. The massive hulks tower over the small fishing boat in the foreground. *Courtesy of Maine Maritime Museum.*

changed occasionally, and new ships were added while others miraculously found work. By the fall of 1930, there were nearly a dozen schooners laid up there. Many were rafted together so they would take up less space. At a time when carriages were being put up in barn lofts for safe keeping, sailing vessels were being similarly stored; they were laid up in rivers, harbors and coves and along unused wharves.

The *Freeman* spent some time in the Ghost Fleet. No stranger to adventure, the four-masted *Freeman*, launched at Rockland, Maine, in 1919, began her career hauling routine cargoes of coal and lumber. In January 1922, with her hold full of coal, she collided with a steamer and lost her forward rigging, needing to be towed in for repair. In October 1922, during Prohibition, the *Freeman* was bound for Bangor, Maine, with another load of coal when she crossed paths with a rumrunner near New York. At this point, the captain is reported to have developed a substantial thirst, trading some of the schooner's stores for a few bottles of "refreshment." This eventually resulted in the captain becoming drunk and coming on deck, taking over the wheel. When he tried to steer the schooner right onto the Long Island shore, the crew pulled him away from the helm and put him in irons. In 1929, after a few other mishaps at sea and waning cargoes, the *Freeman* was laid up in Boothbay Harbor to take her place in the Ghost Fleet. In 1941, she was towed to Nova Scotia, where she suffered the indignity of losing her masts and became a coal barge. She was scuttled in 1947, a worn-out hulk.

The G.G. Deering Company in Bath launched the five-masted *Courtney C. Houck* in 1913, using her successfully in the coasting trade. In 1926, the

The deck of the five-master *Courtney C. Houck* as she lies in Boothbay, tied up to the *Zebedee E. Cliff*. The *Courtney*'s deck is becoming weathered and is in disarray. *Courtesy of Boothbay Region Historical Society.*

*Houck* was sold to Crowell & Thurlow, and she remained under sail until 1929, when she was laid up in the mud at Boothbay Harbor with the Ghost Fleet. Because of her size, it had become difficult to find crews to sail on her and too costly to maintain such a large wooden vessel. The slowly rotting *Houck* was sold again in 1937, but she was never to go back to sea. She was auctioned for scrap, stripped and left to rot.

The story of the four-masted *Edna M. McKnight* is one of particular interest. She was built by R.L. Bean in Camden, Maine, in 1918, and frequently visited the West Indies, as well as the Maritime Provinces. Later, she was operated by Crowell & Thurlow of Boston. The *McKnight* could be a fast boat; she once made it from New Orleans to Boston in nineteen days loaded with molasses. The most interesting story unfolded in the fall of 1926, when the *McKnight*'s master, newly married Captain Alvin Loesche, decided to take his new bride on the vessel for their honeymoon.

Johanna Loesche intended to have a lovely holiday aboard the schooner, visiting different ports and enjoying the romance of being on a beautiful four-masted wind ship with her dashing, seafaring husband. She had taken her trousseau, wedding gifts, linens and silver aboard. In November, the *McKnight* was fully loaded with lumber in Galveston and was making her way toward Boston. Even the deck was piled eight feet high with lumber.

# From Glory Days to Ghost Ships

The Ghost Fleet
lingers at Boothbay,
awaiting the next
voyage, circa 1937.
*Courtesy of Maine
Maritime Museum.*

Somewhere off the coast of Virginia, the ship was struck by a hurricane-force gale. Waves swept over the deck and shifted the lumber, while the crew cut the lashings and sent it overboard. In the terrible punishment, the great schooner's seams began to open, while all four masts were toppled and lost.

The cargo of lumber was the only thing keeping the vessel afloat as she drifted helplessly; soon she was spotted by a British steamer two hundred miles east of Bermuda. The steamer's skipper was reluctant to take the passengers aboard as he had not many provisions himself. Mrs. Loesche left all of her belongings behind except for her cat, which she hid in her blouse. The abandoned, drifting, mastless schooner was eventually located and towed back to Boston, where her cargo was discharged. In September 1927, the battered *Edna M. McKnight* was towed into Boothbay to join the Ghost Fleet.

Two members of the Ghost Fleet were lucky enough to be refitted and sent back out to sea. The beautiful *Helen Barnett Gring*, launched at the Bean Shipyard in Camden in 1919, was reputed to be one of the handsomest and best sailing schooners ever produced in New England. She had her share of storms and collisions during a productive early career, but about 1930, when Crowell & Thurlow could no longer find work for her, she was sent to stay with the Ghost Fleet. Luckily, in 1936 she was refitted and reactivated and enjoyed a brief career as a sailing vessel once more. In 1940, the *Helen Barnett Gring* ran aground and sank on a reef in the West Indies. At least it was an honorable death for a ship.

The *Herbert L. Rawding* was not as lovely as the *Gring*, nor was she a particularly good vessel to sail, notoriously "cranky" and difficult to maneuver when unloaded. The *Rawding* was, however, one of the most well known of sailing vessels in New England and one of the longest lived. Launched in Stockton Springs, Maine, in 1919, the *Rawding* was operated by Crowell &

Hauled as close to shore as she would go, the massive bowsprit and jib boom of a great ghostly schooner overhangs the shore. *Courtesy of Boothbay Region Historical Society.*

Thurlow early in her career. No different than many of her brethren, she joined the ranks of the Ghost Fleet about 1930, and it appeared that she might remain there. Fortunately for the *Rawding*, she was spotted sitting in the Boothbay mud by noted seafarer and entrepreneur Captain Harold Foss. He purchased her in 1937 and sent her to Portland to be refitted with a new spanker mast, repaired and have her bottom scraped. As if that wasn't enough, she had a new suit of sails and was given an auxiliary generator to provide electric lighting. Things worked out for a while, until the end of World War II. In 1946, her topmasts were removed along with her mizzenmast, and she was fitted with two diesel engines that vibrated her seams open within a year. In early June 1947, the *Herbert L. Rawding* took on water and sunk in the Mediterranean.

Another chapter in the saga of the Ghost Fleet is that of V-J Day, or Victory over Japan Day. It was August 14, 1945, and was the event that signaled the end of World War II. In Boothbay Harbor, Maine, it also became known as the day the vessels were burned.

The country had survived yet another world war and had again emerged victorious. Good had triumphed over evil, the oppressed had been liberated and despicable depravity had been put in its place. Certainly a cause for celebration! Somebody was ringing the church bells, horns were honking, musicians were playing, folks were singing and dancing in the streets and strangers were kissing one another! Was this Maine or Times Square? In the evening, the boisterous clamor continued until it bordered on the vulgar and disrespectful. Irreverence is a trait that plagues the youth of all generations, and

# From Glory Days to Ghost Ships

A once noble four-masted schooner, possibly the *Freeman*. Now rotting near shore, she only threatens to ply heavy weeds rather than heavy seas. *Courtesy of Boothbay Region Historical Society.*

it begets the regret that torments us in maturity. During the evening of August 14, 1945, a few young men concocted a plan to set the Ghost Fleet afire! This event is recounted years later by one of the fire-setters in the September 1961 edition of *Maine Coast Fisherman* in an article entitled "We Burned the Vessels":

> *At the time, burning the vessels seemed a perfectly reasonable thing to do. As I look back on it now, destroying the picturesque old relics seems profane. I have developed a veneration for all Maine antiquities, and I would almost as soon be shot as harm them. Of course now I am not looking at things through the eyes of a 15-year-old...alas.*

These irreverent young adults were all too soon destined to become ghosts themselves, forsaken by the generation that was to follow—like the derelict schooners they destroyed. So, too, will we find our place in history!

As years passed, what was left of the Ghost Fleet of old schooners lingered in the Mill Cove at Boothbay until they simply rotted away. Like the Wiscasset Schooners, those at Boothbay also became tourist attractions. Now, even the bones are gone, save just a few, scattered in a heap that can only be seen at low tide.

# The Log of the
# *Zebedee E. Cliff*

I was hoping to find something exceptional at the Boothbay Region Historical Society, some tangible remnant of an age past or something that would breathe life into the story of the schooners. I hoped that there might be a logbook lying around somewhere, but I never imagined that this wish would come to fruition. I hadn't known of the treasures hidden away at the Boothbay Region Historical Society.

Historical society director Barbara Rumsey smiled as she set down an archival box filled with journals and logbooks.

"Here they are," she said. "The logbook from the *Zebedee E. Cliff* is right on top. There is another upstairs in the display case if you are interested. They were removed from the hulk back in the '30s and returned to us over fifty years later."

"You are so lucky to have this," I declared. "Thank you for letting me see it."

"It's what we do," Barbara replied. "We're a museum. It's what we're here for."

I couldn't believe my luck to have actually found a log from one of the Ghost Fleet ships—and of all ships, the *Zebedee E. Cliff*, which now resides at the bottom of Portland Harbor. Fortunately, the logbook didn't go down with it. I looked at the discolored, timeworn item:

*LOG BOOK*
*Schr. Zebedee E. Cliff*
*Boston, Ma*
*Capt. Chas M. Look*

Although it was only eighty years since the log had been written, it somehow seemed as if it had been two hundred years or more. The way of life that was depicted in the log was certainly no stranger to those who were sailors two or three hundred years ago. But to us today, this last age of sail is so foreign and far-removed from our lives that it might as well lie an eternity away.

I carefully picked up the ledger-type clothbound book and opened it; as I did a musty smell emanated from its yellowed pages. I wondered what secrets the book held and how long it had been since they had last been released:

*JOURNAL from NEWPORT NEWS towards CALAIS ME*

The log clearly began with a routine trip from a Newport News, Virginia coal pier to Calais, Maine, to unload the precious commodity so desperately needed in New England. The log begins in October 1930. Just prior to visiting Newport News, the schooner stopped at a fertilizer plant to discharge cargo from Eastport, Maine. The four-masted Maine-built schooner diligently performed the work for which it was intended, well after the end of the age of the sailing vessel. Although it was a routine trip for the *Cliff*, it is far from routine today. The words, although simple, give us a glimpse of what sailing these ships was all about. I have omitted several entries that had "nothing of importance to note" or that I could not read due to illegibility:

*Tuesday, 7th day of October, 1930*

*This day begins with fine weather. The Sch. Zebedee E. Cliff is laying at Chas. W Pride Fertilizer Plant discharging cargo from Eastport, ME beginning at 7am. 4 sailors come aboard. Vessel all discharged 12:30 pm. Left the wharf at 1pm and towed over to Newport News, anchored 4:15 pm. The day ends with fair weather conditions. Pump and lights attended to.*

*Thursday, 9th day of October, 1930*

*This day begins with NE wind and hazy, got on the way 6am and towed in to Newport News. Coal started on board 7am. Soft coal for Calais, ME all loaded 3pm. 2046 tons. The vessel is drawing 21, 10 f. forward 22 f. aft. Towed outside and anchored 35 fathom chain. The day ends clear with NE winds. Pump and lights attended to.*

*Friday, 10th day of October, 1930*

*The day begins with clear weather, NE wind. Noon same. Crew employed in making the vessel ready for sail. Same weather conditions at end of day. Pump and lights attended to.*

*Friday, 17th day of October, 1930*

*Begins hazy with SW wind, all sails set noon calm pass Cape Henry Light, breeze from southward, 4:30 breeze increasing. 11pm squall from NE all light sail and spanker fast, pass Hog Island 11pm. Pump and lights attended to.*

*Saturday, 18th day of October, 1930*

*Begin cloudy and blowing hard, northerly 8am wind NNW. Reef spanker and all sail. Noon clear, 8pm wind NW, the day ends with same weather conditions, pump and lights attended to.*

*Sunday, 19th day of October, 1930*

*Begins fair, WSW-N wind, course NE by N, noon same. 10am wind howling to NNW blowing hard. The vessel is goin [sic] for all sail set with exc. of spanker reefed. Same at end of day. Pump and lights attended to.*

*Monday, 20th day of October, 1930*

*12am begins with cloudy weather and heavy sea and NW strong breeze, sea rising. Mizzen, fore topsail, mizzen topsail torn, all light sail. Heaved to 1am. 8am wind moderating mizzen replaced, other sails repaired and set with exception of fore topsail. Passed Chineakook [sic] 4:30pm pass Montauk 10:30pm. Pump and lights attended to.*

*Wednesday, 22nd day of October, 1930*

*Begins clear, wind NNW, pass Pollack 12:45, Nauset in NW 12 miles of, 5:30am NNW wind and cloudy during forenoon. Crew employed in repairing sail. Noon same weather. 6pm light wind from WNW. Same at end of day. Pump and lights attended to.*

*Thursday, 23rd day of October, 1930*

*Starts with moderate westerly wind. Clear. Noon same, all sails set. 4pm wind SW Monhegan in NNW 10 miles of 11:30pm. Pump and lights attended to.*

*Friday, 24th day of October, 1930*

*Begins cloudy SSW wind, pass Metinicous [sic] 4am. 8am wind checking to south. Strong SSE-S.Easterly wind. Kept off for Bar Harbor anchored there 4pm 90 fath chain. Day ends with NE rainstorm, 8pm paid out all the chain on starb. Anchor. Pump and lights attended to.*

*Saturday, 25th day of October, 1930*

*This day begins with E-NE storm and heavy rainsqualls noon. Same at end of day. Pump and lights attended to.*

*Sunday, 26th day of October, 1930*

*Begins with northerly wind blowing hard. Weather clearing. Noon same. 5:30pm got on the way, set lower sails, reef spanker and all jibs, pass Egg Rk 7:30pm, same weather at end of day. Pump and lights attended to.*

*Friday, 31st day of October, 1930*

*Begins cloudy with NE wind, mate and boatswain employed in repairing sails, noon clear calm, same at end of day. Pump and lights attended to.*

*Friday, 7th day of November, 1930*

*Begins clear. NW gale, freezing. Noon same. 5pm got on the way and towed down to Devils Ledge, anchored there 10pm. Wind moderating at end of day. Pump and lights attended to.*

*Saturday, 8th day of November, 1930*

*On account of low tide unable to go in to coal pier, nothing else of importance to note.*

*Sunday, 9th day of November, 1930*

*Begins with cloudy weather and SW wind. Got on the way 9am and towed in to Calais and made fast to the coal pier at noon. Same weather at end of day, pumps attended.*

*Monday, 10th day of November, 1930*

*Begin discharging coal from 7am to 4pm, 9 hours. Pumps attended.*

*Tuesday, 11th day of November, 1930*

*Begins with fair weather. Freezing. Discharging 9 hours. Pumps attended.*

*Saturday, 15th day of November, 1930*

*Discharging cargo 7am to 12noon. All cargo out. Pumps attended. 1 sailor came aboard.*

*Monday, 17th day of November, 1930*

*This day begins calm, hazy. Left the coal pier at 7:30am and towed down to Eastport, anchored there at noon, stb. anchor 90 fathom chain. Pump and lights attended.*

*Tuesday, 18th day of November, 1930*

*Begin with Easterly wind and hazy. 2 sailors came aboard. Men employed in shifting sails.*

*Thursday, 20th day of November, 1930*

*Begins hazy w winds. Got on the way and towed in to the beach at the Saltsworks, 1 sailor came aboard and 2 extra men was [sic] hired to scrape the bottom, scraped at low water from 1pm to 5pm.*

*Friday, 21st day of November, 1930*

*This day begins five crew and hired men employed in overhauling the bottom. The vessel broke a water pipe going across the deck.*

*Saturday, 22nd day of November, 1930*

*Continuing on the bottom 5am, wind SW strong 10am, got towboat and towed out 12:30pm, the vessel doing some minor damage on the wharfs. The day ends with SW wind, vessel anchored off Eastport, lights and pumps attended to.*

The first log entry ends at this point, and on the next page it begins again:

*JOURNAL from CALAIS ME towards HAMPTON ROADS*

It is clear that the schooner was frequently traveling back and forth from coal ports in the Mid-Atlantic, delivering the cargo to points in Maine and returning with whatever she could. Hampton Roads and Newport News were busy coal ports. It is interesting to note that although it only took one day to load the coal in Virginia, it took six days to unload it in Calais, Maine. The voyage from Virginia to Maine took four weeks, and the crew did hit some really bad weather on Monday, October 20 when they "heaved to" and rode out the storm.

It was also noted when a new sailor came aboard, often when the ship was lying at the dock or coal pier. A ship's crew was constantly changing, some coming on board and others leaving. The ship's master would change from time to time as well or even from one voyage to another. The following is an excerpt from the log describing another trip back to Maine from a coal pier. The master is a "Captain Publicover," probably Wilson Publicover, who had captained the *Cliff* before. This excerpt is notable because during the voyage the captain became ill and was eventually taken off the ship by the Coast Guard and subsequently hospitalized on December 26. The excerpt is from the trip that was already underway:

*JOURNAL from NEWPORT NEWS towards BATH, ME*

*Saturday, 13th day of December, 1930*

*Begins with NE winds, crew employed in repairing sails. Captain sick. Same weather at end of day. Pump and lights attended to.*

*Tuesday, 16th day of December, 1930*

*Starts with NE wind. Master still sick. Crew employed in various work on deck. Same wind at end of day. Pump and lights attended to.*

*Wednesday, 17th day of December, 1930*

*This day begins with strong NE wind and snow. Brought Docktor [sic] aboard for the Master. Strong NE gale at end of day. Pump and lights attended to.*

*Thursday, 18th day of December, 1930*

*Begins with NE storm, 8am moderating. 4:30pm wind light NW. Got on the way. Anchored in the edge of Newport News. Pump and lights attended to.*

*Wednesday, 24th day of December, 1930*

*Begin with fresh wind NW by N, pass Hog Island 3am. Wind WNW gale, outer jib taken in and spanker reefed, pass Fenwick [sic] lightship 1pm. Gale increasing, snow squall, reefed fore, main, mizzen. Pass North East end Lightship 6:30pm. Wind NNW decreasing at end of day. Pump and lights attended to. Captain still sick.*

*Thursday, 25th day of December, 1930*

*Begins with strong NNW wind. Set full, fore, main, mizzen. 6am moderate NW wind. Set outer jib and mizzen tops. All sails set 8am. The Master is very sick. Decided to go for New York, anchored 10:30 3 miles ENE of Ambrose Lightship. Starb. Anchor 90 fath chain. Pump and lights attended.*

*Friday, 26th day of December, 1930*

*This day begins with WSW wind, 8am hoist up signals for the Coast Guard Lightship. Noon calm. 3:30 lowered boat and went to Ambrose Lightship and sent a message for the rev. cutter. 5:00 Coast Guard patrol boat took Capt. to Hospital. The day end with fresh ENE breeze. Pump and lights and watch on deck carefully attended to.*

*Monday, 29th day of December, 1930*

*This day begins with NW wind and clear weather. Crew employed repairing bob chain and other things on deck. Noon wind W by N, weather cloudy. 3:30 Capt. Publicover came aboard, got on way. Pass Fire Island Lightship 10pm. Pump and lights attended.*

The four-masted *Zebedee E. Cliff* and five-masted *Courtney C. Houck* aground and tied up to each other, awaiting an uncertain fate. *Courtesy of Boothbay Region Historical Society.*

In 1932, while still in good condition but unable to find work, the *Zebedee E. Cliff* was laid up at Boothbay Harbor. She worked off and on, managing to find an occasional coal delivery, but by 1937 it was clear that she would likely become a permanent resident of the Ghost Fleet. In 1941, the *Cliff*, along with the *Maude M. Morey*, was towed to Portland Harbor and scuttled for use as a breakwater and anti-submarine defense. Perhaps she is still there.

I looked out of the window at the setting sun and carefully placed the long-forgotten logbook back into the box from which it had come earlier that day. Certainly the sailors who had written the words on the yellowed pages nearly eighty years prior never suspected that somebody in the twenty-first century would be reading them.

On my return trip, now heading south on U.S. Route 1, I crossed the bridge that ran over the Sheepscot River and into Wiscasset. I looked over to the left, where the schooners used to be; all I saw were pieces of a rotting wharf reaching out to nothing but emptiness.

I parked my truck across from the Wiscasset Old General Store, right near the old docks, and began to walk along the shore as I had when I would visit the old ships. Despite the fact that I knew they were gone, I looked for them anyway. A new dock had been built with a large platform overlooking the river. I scrambled up onto it and again looked over to where the schooners had been. I looked down and saw nothing but seaweed being washed gently against the pier stanchions, and then I looked up at the empty expanse of saltwater that stretched, I knew, to the sea.

The *Luther Little* lies with her bow ports open to the sea, circa 1970s. *Courtesy of Lawrence Lufkin.*

Now, even the Wiscasset Schooners are gone. I visited the Wiscasset Old General Store to buy a postcard depicting the famous ships, as I did as a child and later as a young adult. I slowly spun the revolving racks that were filled with postcards, looking for a picture of the schooners. Finally, after looking through the third and final rack, I found my prize, a color photo taken of the hulks in the evening, during a nearly full moon. As I pulled the treasure from its slot, my heart began to beat a little more quickly. Clutching the object tightly in my fingers, as if I could momentarily capture what it portrayed, I smiled, walked to the cash register and set my treasure down.

The store clerk, an older man with graying hair, looked puzzled. "Is that all, ma'am?" he asked.

"Yes," I replied, proudly.

"That will be thirty-two cents," he said, matter-of-factly.

"That's all? Just thirty-two cents?" I asked. "Somehow it just doesn't seem like enough. The schooners are gone now."

The huge six-masted *Wyoming* under sail for the first time on the Kennebec, heading out to sea. *Courtesy of Maine Maritime Museum.*

"Yup. They're gone, but they were sure somethin' while they were here. Those ships were quite a thing in these parts. Everybody came to see 'em."

"All that's left are these postcards. It's a shame," I replied glumly.

"Don't even know about the postcards," the clerk said. "After these go, I don't even know if I can get any more. They'll be gone too, soon enough."

And so it is that often we don't realize what we have until it is gone—until it becomes "history." It is comforting to know, however, that if we can't capture it and hold it for all time at least we are aware that it existed. We are able to understand it, to comprehend it fully and to document what we have known.

Many maritime authors see no value in the story of the last schooners; the large post–nineteenth century hulks just aren't romantic. I don't agree. Sometimes, the way a thing ends is much more moving and meaningful than the way it began. It was not only the Wiscasset Schooners that seemed to be attempting to defy fate, their massive gray hulks lying open to the sea and waiting beside docks that had long since rotted away and now just resembled bones sticking up out of the water. It seemed as if all of the large coastal schooners, even in their heyday, were tangible evidence of our reluctance to let go of an era—in this case the age of sail. The schooners clung stubbornly, a reflection not of the ships but instead of the people who pushed them. In this way, the schooners become even more romantic than the most beautiful square-rigged vessels and storied whaling ships. We see ourselves in the schooners, as well as all that is honorable in humanity.

# Bibliography

Asbury, Herbert. *Carry Nation: The Woman with the Hatchet*. New York: Alfred A. Knopf, 1929.

Bacheldor, Peter Dow. *Shipwrecks & Maritime Disasters of the Maine Coast*. Portland, ME: Provincial Press, 1997.

*Boothbay Register*. "Abandoned Schooner Edna McKnight." April 24, 1980.

*Boston Advertiser*, September 20, 1880.

Bowker, Francis E. *Hull-Down*. New Bedford, MA: Reynolds-DeWalt, 1963.

Bradbury, James E. *Seafarers of Somerset*. N.p., 1996.

Burgess, Robert H. *Sea, Sails and Shipwreck*. Cambridge, MD: Tidewater Publishers, 1970.

Currier, Isabel. "The 'Edna Hoyt'." *Down East* (June 1964).

Duncan, Roger F. *Coastal Maine: A Maritime History*. New York: W.W. Norton & Company, 1992.

*Fall River Evening News*, 1917 and 1918. Located at Fall River Public Library, Fall River, Massachusetts, microfilm.

Gaddis, Vincent. *Invisible Horizons: True Mysteries of the Sea*. New York: Chilton Books, 1965.

Haskell, Loren E. "The Glamorous Six-Masters." *Down East* (April 1965).

Hunt, James W. "The Four-Masted Schooners of Boothbay Harbor." Part 1. *Nautical Research Journal* 43 (1998): 211–18.

———. "The Four-Masted Schooners of Boothbay Harbor." Part 2. *Nautical Research Journal* 44, no. 1 (1999): 23–34.

———. "The Four-Masted Schooners of Boothbay Harbor." Part 3. *Nautical Research Journal* 44, no. 2 (1999): 89–98.

Jones, Robert C., and David L. Register. *Two Feet to Tidewater*. Boulder, CO: Pruett Publishing, 1987.

Kingsbury, Henry D., and Simeon L. Deyo. *History of Kennebec County, Maine*. New York: H.W. Blake & Company, 1892.

Lewis, Gerald E. "We Burned the Vessels." *National Fisherman: Maine Coast Fisherman* (September 1961): 24–26.

MacGregor, David R. *The Schooner: Its Design and Development from 1600 to the Present*. Annapolis, MD: Naval Institute, 1997.

McMaster, John Bach. *The United States in the World War*. New York: D. Appleton and Company, 1920.

Morey, David C. *The Voyage of Archangell: James Rosier's Account of the Waymouth Voyage of 1605*. Gardiner, ME: Tilbury House Publishers, 2005.

*New York Times*, December 17, 1888; January 24, 1910; June 6, 1918; and July 24, 1918.

Parker, W.J. Lewis, Captain. "The Gov. Ames." *Down East* (July 1970): 48–52.

Perry, Lawrence. *Our Navy in the War*. New York: Charles Scribner's Sons, 1919.

Pohl, William. "The Way It Was." *Down East* (August 1978): 78–80.

Rice, George Wharton. *The Shipping Days of Old Boothbay*. 1938. Reprint, Somersworth, NH: New England History Press, 1984, in collaboration with the Boothbay Region Historical Society.

Roy, M. Chris. *The Wiscasset Ships: A Remembrance*. Westport Island, ME: Pumpkin Press, 1994.

Schiffer, Michael. *Anthropological Perspectives on Technology*. Dragoon, AZ: Amerind Foundation, 2001.

Simpson, Bland. *Ghost Ship of Diamond Shoals: The Mystery of the Carroll A. Deering*. Chapel Hill: University of North Carolina Press, 2002.

Snow, Edward Rowe. *Great Gales and Dire Disasters*. New York: Dodd, Mead and Company, 1952.

Snow, Ralph Linwood, and Douglas K. Lee, Captain. *A Shipyard in Maine: Percy & Small and the Great Schooners*. Gardiner, ME: Tilbury House Publishers, 1999.

Stevens, James P., Jr. "Boothbay Schooners." *Down East* (September 1968): 34–39.

Tod, Giles M.S. *The Last Sail Down East*. Barre, MA: Barre Publishers, 1965.

United States Office of Naval Records and Library. *German Submarine Activities on the Atlantic Coast of the United States and Canada*. Washington, D.C.: Government Printing Office, 1920.

Williamson, Joseph. *History of the City of Belfast in the State of Maine*. Boston, MA: Houghton Mifflin Company, 1913.

Zebedee E. Cliff Logbook, courtesy of the Boothbay Region Historical Society.

# About the Author

As a child growing up in a 1799 farmhouse in rural Maine, Ingrid Grenon was surrounded by history. She lived and breathed it. She loved hearing stories about her *Mayflower* ancestors, who were both Saints and Strangers. She listened intently as she was told about those who fought in the Revolutionary War and about a great-great-great-grandfather who joined the Sixty-first Maine Infantry during the Civil War. She is also very proud of her great-great-great-grandfather, Captain William Peachey, who was lost at sea when his schooner sunk near Portland Harbor during a gale in December 1876. She learned, too, of a Sebago Indian from whom she is descended. These are the things that impressed her from a young age.

*Photo courtesy of April Rossi.*

Currently employed by the Commonwealth of Massachusetts, Grenon has a degree in psychology and a riding master's degree. She is a member of the Maine Maritime Museum, Boothbay Region Historical Society and the Hill-Stead Museum. She is also a published poet.

Visit us at
www.historypress.net